MW00636321

There's a Skunk in My Tent!

STUART CHAPPELL

To DAN ?

Stu

Table of Contents

LIFE IS AN ADVENTURE

I received my formal education at Western Michigan University. I've been a schoolteacher, taxidermist, woodcarver, outfitter, dabbler in real estate, and a traveler throughout the U.S.A., Canada and Mexico. I've been a blue-collar worker in factories, run a business and raised a family; but I've learned more about life from the outdoors than any other source. Some have been hard lessons.

Why is one drawn to nature's school time and again, so as to put ourselves through some very rigorous assignments? Allow me to share some of these stories and personal visions, and you will see why.

To be afforded a daily view of the Rocky Mountains, I moved to Colorado in 1972. I chose this scene rather than the shadowed, starless canyon lands of an eastern metropolis because a major, though unaccredited, factor in all our lives is the land. The land, so vast, so promising, so dangerous, still pre-occupies our people and shapes our character just as it did for people of earlier times. Most of us live on a piece of real estate which is not only formed as the result of plate tectonics, but also of an equally titanic force: the visions of the generations who came before us, and the actions they took in accord with those visions.

My first deer taken by shotgun in Allegan Co., Michigan.

The challenge of adventure brings many visitors to the mountains, and adventure is there waiting for you. But your enjoyment of the outdoors depends on the right attitude. Whether you are a hunter being guided, or a guide with a hunter (I've been both) attitude is ninety percent of the experience. While some folks grumble about adversity, others in the very same situation will have an enlightening experience.

Two important factors in enjoying the outdoors are our degree of preparedness and the packing issue: light and fast or loaded and slow. It is the persistent dilemma of backcountry enjoyment. The pace of modern business tempts many people to travel lightly. They want to cover a lot of territory on a limited schedule. Travel too light and you may suddenly find you're missing a key element for survival. Conversely, an overloaded pack can turn a simple jaunt into an endurance contest. The

I caught this five-pound bass in high school at Hopkins, Michigan.

average person forgets that nature is very powerful and not always kind. Pack for the worst and hope for the best, always. The following adventures make my point.

A Wyoming hunt in 1967.

Survival Elk Hunt

It was October 10, 1978, the day before Colorado's rifle season for elk opened. Perkins, Jerry and his fourteen year-old son Todd, and I set out from our ranch, eight miles south of Montrose. We drove three hours through some of the most beautiful scenery the Rocky Mountains can offer—high peaks where the road twists up the sheer sides of the mountains. This range is so steep that roads can't go straight up; they are a series of switchbacks without guardrails, the narrow shoulders dropping off into space. I could glance back at my horse trailer and see an ant-like procession of other vehicles hundreds of feet below.

The last town we went through was the former mining boomtown of Silverton, where gold miners would come to spend their "poke" once a month, and then go back to the hills for more. We stopped to put our trucks in four-wheel drive and started the steeper climb on an unimproved jeep track to the trailhead. Boulders had slid into the so-called road, and every so often we would stop and lever them out of the way as we made slow progress to the road's end at an abandoned gold mine, the Maggie Gulch trailhead.

We packed the horses with our gear, mounted and started up the trail. Our destination was over the Continental Divide to the east on a sheep trail along the West Fork of Pole Creek, about a three and a half hour ride, if all went well. The sun

Silverton, Colorado.

brightened the cloudless noonday sky and dissolved new patches of snow into smaller and smaller clumps. The air was cool, but our bodies savored the sun's warmth. The brown grass still glistened with moisture and gave off a pungent freshness as the dew evaporated. Life was good!

An appreciation for the whims of mountain weather is always in the back of my mind.. I have come to think that the last to know the true forecast are snakes and our television weatherpersons. As we topped the Divide I remembered how

Going in on a very pleasant day.

the valley looked when I scouted it earlier, the trees ablaze with color. Now only the green of spruce and fur broke the brown of grass and leafless limbs. Winter seemed to be coming early to the high-country.

We came off the Divide and entering the dark timber, a favorite haunt of elk. My hopes rose as soon as we were in the dark woods; thirty yards of fresh tracks appeared along a lower trail. Elk may spend many days making footprints while circling round for miles and miles, but not in this country. The strip timber bunches the herd into a smaller area where there is plenty of feed and plenty of cover, but each territory is clearly marked off by such paths. I knew this would be a memorable hunt.

Camp at timberline.

We entered a clearing at 11,500 feet, the upper edge of the timber, and made camp. Unloading all the things that make camp comfortable is a time when you really appreciate your horses. There were droppings from other horses, and I looked at them to determine how the animals were being used. A traveling horse leaves its droppings strung out along a trail. A sheep herder's horse, being able to stop at will, leaves its in a pile. These were a single pile, so the droppings were not a sign that someone else had scouted the area recently.

Sitting around the campfire that evening, enjoying the way it mellows the night's chill and keeps good quiet company, I smiled to myself. Although I had often hunted alone in years past, I believe easy-going hunting partners are key to nearly all our recollections—memorable things happen when good buddies are present. Many respect an aptitude for hunting and the skills developed in pursuit of it, but the killing of game is not the measure of a hunt's enjoyment. Most outdoor adventures do not make suitable stories for magazines, which need close calls and miraculous endings. Usually the actual hunting experience is simple and personal. Still, hunting and fishing with our children and friends and learning the character-building lessons that nature teaches us are reason enough for being out here.

The next morning we placed Todd, the boy, in a meadow below the strip timber and told him to wait for elk to cross, while Jerry, Perkins and I went up to hunt the trails meandering through the timber. I instructed Todd not to approach a wounded elk unless he knew it was finished. A mature bull elk can be brought down by a dart loaded with two c.c.'s of tranquilizer, if it is calm; but energized and chased, it can take eighteen c.c.'s to bring the same bull down. Never chase a wounded animal. Let it go, then follow it after a thirty-minute wait. Otherwise you can push it for miles.

A bright morning with a pure transparent atmosphere bathed my heart with gladness as we worked up the mountain. Reaching the woods, the two other men split off, each taking a separate way in. I climbed on through pretty country, which varied between dark woods and open majestic views. Was it the usual lonesome feeling, or was something else weighing at the back of my neck? I couldn't be lonesome; I had three buddies and a string of horses in this valley.

I crossed the footprints of a coyote, which I recognized by its larger forefeet; a dog's feet are all the same size. Tracks are amusing. Elk cross open spaces, climb up steep inclines, even up slide-rock, but seldom take a trail up a draw. They go wherever they want. I have seldom followed tracks to game, unless I just wanted to move them for other hunters, my partners preferably. I leave tracking to Hollywood Indians and dogs.

Ruminants, like elk, can consume only two and a half percent of their body weight in dry feed per day. They have twelve to thirteen hours grazing time in which to do it, the remaining time being used for travel, rest and cud chewing. Though nature has equipped elk with a most efficient and adaptable digestive system, allowing them to eat most anything available, all elk have a critical feeding season. In the fall they must develop their kidney fat capsule; it cannot be developed at any other season. Only a good fat reserve enables the animal to survive severe winter conditions.

The country began to open around me as I climbed toward timberline. I found an inviting fallen tree and sat for a moment to rest and absorb my surroundings. Mountains bring more than the fragrance of spruce and the drama of peaks rising above 14,000 feet; they have a psychological as well as an aesthetic impact. My musing was cut short by a crashing sound coming from downhill behind me. I turned to watch glimpses of hide and antler climbing out of the steep bowl whose rim I sat near.

Through the scope I could make out five ivory tips to each side of the bull's bobbing rack. He was closing fast. At a hundred yards I thumbed off the safety and squeezed the trigger.

Myself, with a good bull. Todd, the 14 year old boy, took this bull.

I've always shot a .270 with hand-loaded spear point 130-grain bullets. Most people say it's too small a load for elk; but it's not if you hit where you aim. In twenty-seven years of hunting, no elk I shot at has been lost once it was hit, though I've missed my share. I am convinced that most hunters over-gun themselves.

The bull dropped where it stood. While cleaning it I heard shots from the valley below and then to my left. I hoped they were from our party.

In camp that night we were a happy group of hunters, the boy and his father each having shot bulls. The next day we planned an early haul out. Jerry had to be in Grand Junction that night, so he and I would pack out the two elk and I'd go back for the gear and the others, since the rest of us had more time.

It was clear and cold as we started out of the valley, but Rocky Mountain weather is fast moving and unpredictable. Each region has its own climate, and anomalies occur where

We were ready to pull out.

topography controls the weather. We hadn't been gone long before the snow was falling so thick we couldn't see the trail. All we knew was we were going up. We must have crossed the Divide because the storm broke into full snowy bloom. The wind swept past in hissing floods, throwing icy crystals up as well, blasting our faces. Flakes, which had been ground to a fine dust, dimmed the light to an icy gloom. We began to wonder, what if we were caught in a whiteout, at the mercy of bone-gnawing wind-chill?

All one can do at this point is rely on the senses of your horse; they can somehow feel the trail under the snow and know where they're going. Sheba, the horse I was riding, was familiar with these mountain trails, as she had been roaming them since she was a foal.

After three and a half hour's of riding, we were back at the vehicles. Though he didn't say anything, I knew Jerry was worried about his son back at camp. I had to go in for him. The return trip would be faster leading three horses with the wind at our back most of the time.

When I rode into camp I told Perkins to fix me a cup of coffee and get ready; we were taking Todd back to his dad.

"We haven't time to break camp, pack up the other elk and get the boy back before dark," he reasoned. "Better that you two move fast and light; and Stu, you come back in the morning for me and the gear."

The blizzard commenced in deadly earnest as we made our way up the east side of the Divide. The horses worked their way uphill on what we hoped was the trail, but they were digging and pawing, slipping and sliding, sometimes down on their knees, even pulling with their noses at times. I kept calling encouragement; I couldn't keep from it. I knew these ponies would carry a rider until they froze to death.

Our progress was slow and darkness had set in. Sheba stopped moving, and I peered out from my scarf. We had covered all of our skin—even our eyes. I could see with my flashlight that she was stopped by chest-deep snow.

A string deep inside me started to unravel. It was an important one, the one that ties down panic. I'd heard of people who could not find themselves, who knew neither in nor out, up nor down. They didn't know who they were, much less where they left their senses. I should have kept the boy in camp. We couldn't see and had no idea where we were or what direction to go. One wrong turn and we could go seventy-four miles before finding a road. Visibility was one foot in front of our faces with freezing wind scalding our eyes.

"Are we on the trail?" the boy hollered, as he did each time we stopped; and I hollered back, "Yep!"

We were both exhausted; at such times even the most avid hunter wishes he'd stayed at home.

Sheba backed up and went downhill, working her way

17

on the edge of a canyon where the snow blowing over the edge was not so deep. Up we went again, and as long as she was moving, we were at least going somewhere. The pass over the Continental Divide was a notch about sixty feet across; we had to find that opening. The horses kept moving and we just hung on.

Suddenly we started down. Though riding blind, I could feel my weight shift; I still had no idea where we were headed—maybe back toward camp.

After two more hours, the wind stopped, and we were in thick pines. Hope flickered like a candle flame within me. We could be on the other side, headed for the trailer. Another hour of hanging on, and there we were at the vehicles. Sitting in the truck with the heater roaring, drinking cold coffee and eating frozen sandwiches, I said a little prayer to thank the Lord.

The ordeal wasn't over yet, though Jerry and Todd were on their way back to Grand Junction. I had to sleep in the back of my pickup in a camper shell and ride back in the morning to get Jerry, if he wasn't frozen stiff. About four in the morning I awoke, not so much from cold (because I was snug in side two sleeping bags, one inside the other) but a can of Pepsi lying in a pail of feed had burst, ripped open by the freezing temperature. It had been ten below zero in Silverton that night, and we had been up 4,000 feet higher, in fifty mile an hour winds, all of which made a chill factor of minus seventy degrees!

By daybreak I was trapped inside the camper shell as condensation had solidified in the latch, and the door was frozen shut. I worked on the door with my hunting knife and scratched and chipped my way out into a frigid morning, but at least the snow had stopped falling. After saddling up the horses I had to cut their lead ropes from the trailer, because they were frozen so stiff I couldn't untie them.

I mused that this would be a hunt that would be remembered for all its mistakes. A feeling that I might be going crazy came over me as I laughed at the freezing temperatures, mocking the gnawing cold. I never figured I'd make it out, and I certainly didn't think I'd be going back in these conditions. I don't know what I expected; maybe I should have thought more about it.

I started back up to the Continental Divide, again paralleling the mountain, trying to follow the trail in the snow left by Sheba the night before. I pushed the horses along pretty hard but switched mounts every fifteen minutes so as to break trail for the others.

A Forest Service helicopter came by and with a bullhorn warned me of a major early snowstorm in the mountains and pointed out that I was headed the wrong way to get out fast. Was I OK, they asked, as they watched the horses going berserk.

"I would be if you will just go away and quit spooking the horses," I hollered. I quieted the horses and then thought, "Why hadn't I asked them to pick up my buddy?" Sometimes the brain works too slow too reorganize your priorities.

Finally arriving at camp, I found Perkins stoking the fire as he had all night. "Were you worried?" I asked

That afternoon.

COOLING POWER OF WIND ON EXPOSED FLESH

ESTIMATED WIND SPEED (MPH)	ACTUAL THERMOMETER READING (°F)											
	50	40	30	20	10	0	–10	–20	–30	–40	–50	–60
	EQUIVALENT TEMPERATURE (°F)											
calm	50	40	30	20	10	0	–10	–20	–30	–40	–50	–60
5	48	37	27	16	6	–5	–15	–26	–36	–47	–57	–88
10	40	28	16	4	–9	–21	–33	–46	–58	–70	–83	–95
15	36	22	9	–5	–18	–36	–45	–58	–72	–85	–99	–112
20	32	18	4	–10	–25	–39	–53	–67	–82	–96	–110	–124
25	30	16	0	–15	–29	–44	–59	–74	–88	–104	–118	–133
30	28	13	–2	–18	–33	–48	–63	–79	–94	–109	–125	–140
35	27	11	–4	–20	–35	–40	–67	–82	–98	–113	–129	–145
40	26	10	–6	–21	–37	–53	–69	–85	–100	–116	–132	–148

LITTLE DANGER (for properly clothed person)	INCREASING DANGER	GREAT DANGER

DANGER FROM FREEZING OF EXPOSED FLESH

"No, I knew you would be back."

"Yep," I said, "I was thinking, sometime in the spring, maybe as early as April."

After coffee, we rode out leaving everything—elk, tent and camping gear. We just wanted to get out before the wind came up and trapped us. We made it out, and a week later a stretch of mild weather gave us the chance to ride back in and retrieve the camp. The elk was frozen solid and the coyotes hadn't even got to it. We packed everything out and called it an adventure.

The only lasting effects of the trip were a slightly frozen left side of my face, where the skin turned black and peeled off, and a lifelong appreciation of Sheba, God's own gift of a horse who saved us. Also a realization and perhaps some wisdom: the trump cards are always in the hands of the elements!

Back in the next day to get Perkins.

The Challenge

People often ask me about the possible unpleasant situations that anyone who deals with the public might encounter. What is it like in the wilderness with armed strangers who might have a little to much to drink, or become in some way unbalanced, or are just plain ornery? Outfitters meet some of the best people we have in this country, sportsmen; but, in all honesty, there are some exceptions. Let me share only one situation that illustrates the exception, though hunters with an attitude have surfaced on many occasions.

My partner and I had set up a hunt for a group of folks from the south. They had the option of riding from Silverton, Colorado to the camp over Stony Pass (the Continental Divide), but it would involve hauling nine horses from the ranch south of Montrose, meeting a truck with gear at Pole Creek and then packing and riding it all into camp. Another possibility was to haul only three packhorses to Pole Creek and the hunters would walk over the divide into camp with the horses carrying the gear and supplies. The difference would show up in the cost of the service package. After much discussion, they chose the second package at a more reasonable price. All in the group felt they were in good physical shape, and that the hike would help get them acclimated to the altitude.

The hunt had been set months in advance, but many things can change over time. In this case the ramrod of the group reordered his priorities when he got the opportunity to hunt the Chama Ranch, an exclusive hunt that people wait years for. He chose Harry, a cohort from work, to fill his place in our hunt. Nobody in the group knew much about him, since he had never been a member of their usual hunting party. This annual gathering of men were ready to enjoy their outdoor experience, as refreshing and reassuring as hot coffee. And after working in the cold, competitive business world, they were all looking forward to some recreation.

The day finally arrived for the hunt, and we met all the participants. The last minute replacement turned out to be crabbier than a constipated bear. If I were asked what one thing impressed me as characteristic of that hunt, it would be Harry's untiring ability to find something negative in any situation. I thank Harry for some of the finest complaining I have ever heard. This humorless excuse for a man brought his own supply of four bananas a day for potassium and only wanted hot water for his bouillon cubes. Says he: "I have neither the habit, nor the inclination to eat your greasy meals or put up with any bullshit."

On our way into the backcountry we would travel out of Silverton up the Stony Pass road, toward the headwaters of the Rio Grande River. The Stony Pass trail climbs 3000 feet in three-quarters of a mile (as the crow flies, six miles as the jeep crawls through switch-backs) to trackless, barren tundra above the tree line. Nearby Pole Mountain is a dreary promontory, but is also excellent elk habitat.

Going over the Divide at Stoney Pass.

During the drive to Silverton, Harry, sitting behind me, explained to the other hunters, "This is not elk country. I've hunted Montana, Wyoming and Colorado, and this doesn't look like elk country. Outfitters take you on a hunt and try to entertain you, but it's just a business to them. They don't always get you into the good elk country."

He was talking about me!

I am not proud of the following events, but a man must react to situations as he sees fit. I see a part of my job as keeping up morale on a hunt.

When we arrived at Pole Creek, I suggested to my partner that it was getting late in the day, and he should pack the horses and take the hunting party up the trail (about a two and a half hour trek) to the campsite. I announced loudly that Harry, being in pretty good shape and I would secure the base camp and follow along later. He puffed up like a big dog and sulked off.

The party loaded up and took off with all Harry's stuff on the horses, heading for the camp that was already set up. Intentionally I took my time, stowing gun cases in the van, picking up trash from the food loaded in the panniers, and locking everything in the trucks. When I was satisfied it was getting dark, Harry and I started up the trail. I carried our only light, a large Mag, to show the path. As we hiked along I explained, "It's going to be a cold night, Bud, bitter cold. Yep at 12,200 ft. elevation in mid-October it gets mighty cold."

Not long on the trail Harry started in again. "This is the craziest hunt I've ever been on; I've never walked into camp in my life. This is the cheapest hunting trip, with the dumbest outfitter I ever heard of."

Biting my tongue at first, then with great patience, I explained, "This is the package the group chose; it is what they wanted in order to keep the cost reasonable."

Harry didn't let up, and I kept thinking, "Nature is always there, the great equalizer, strong, relentless, unyielding, triumphant, but she can be your friend. Perhaps I should let her destroy him, then burn him, then bury the ashes in an unmarked grave."

We had to ford Pole Creek, so in my pack I had garbage bags to use as temporary waders, but I decided not to get them out. Approaching the creek I told Harry, "Watch me. You have to jump from rock to rock to get across without getting wet." I shined the light ahead spotting the rocks and hopped along, about fifteen feet to the other side.

I shined the light back and hollered across to Harry, "Make sure you place your foot solidly on the first rock there, and once you get started, you gotta keep right on. Don't stop!" Harry started across, and when he was about midway, I pulled the light and started up the trail. I didn't turn until I heard the splash and yells of abuse. Stopping, I turned and exclaimed, "Sorry, I thought you were across," and then kept walking.

Now Harry was mad. I could picture dripping water starting to make little icicles on his eyebrows and hat brim, but I just kept moving. A few more yards down the trail we had to ford West Pole Creek. Again I admonished, "Watch your step and look for the rock in front where you aim to place your foot next." I demonstrated, bebopping across the stream. As I held the light, Harry started hopping across. Again I pulled the light away. The splashing started and torrents of abuse pierced the night.

As I proceeded on the trail, I heard him running up behind me. Pivoting around, I shined the light in his face, and he stopped. He took a breath through clenched teeth and

Pole Creek, which is much wider with the snow off it.

hissed, " All right, I get it. Don't mess with a man in *his* territory. Right?"

I just said, "OK."

The rest of the walk was uneventful; we traversed a small meadow and then hiked up the hill where I could look down on the cozy glow of the campfire. As I arrived in camp a little ahead of Harry, my partner, Jerry, handed me a mug of coffee.

"Just tell me, is he alive or dead."

"He will be the best judge of that," I replied.

Down the hill came Harry, frozen pants crackling as he walked. The other members of the party saw Harry come into the light like the abominable iceman, but they just turned to their tents or hunkered down by the fire, and none said a word.

"What if he'd a picked up a rock and hit you over the head?" Jerry asked, in a quiet aside.

"I thought of that, and he probably did too. But, where was he? Where was he going? If Harry had not stopped griping,

Up the trail they went with all our gear.

we would still be walking—all night if that's what it took."

Harry kept his comments mostly to himself for the rest of the hunt, though he never would eat our food. It was a gratifying adventure. The hunt went fine, and all the members filled their tags, even Harry, a lesson in negative reinforcement.

Back at Pole Creek trailhead.

Bears

What do you do if you meet a bear? You probably won't, since there are fifty times more chances of having a driving accident on the way to your destination than confronting a bear in the wild. Black bears rarely attack humans, but if you think you can escape one climbing up a tree, think again. They are agile tree climbers.

In Colorado male blacks emerge from their dens during the last two weeks of April. Females generally come out in May, usually the first two weeks of the month, but mothers with newborn cubs are the last to emerge. Females also tend to enter their dens earlier, beginning in October. These factors mean females are less likely than males to meet folks during the spring and fall. Bears in other states may spend much less time in their dens.

Now, if you are looking for bears, or living in their territory, you should consider their eating habits. Bears, like humans, are omnivores—creatures that feed on both animal and vegetable sources—though carrion and freshly caught animals account for only ten percent of a bear's diet. Nuisance complaints about bears are more frequent in late summer and fall, when bears spend twenty hours a day eating. I believe the best time to hunt bear is the second season of elk hunting, and the place—over a previous season's gut pile. The chance of finding a bear by walking around the woods is pretty slim. After

Yellowstone bears in
July, 1966.

spending half of my life in the outdoors, summer and fall, I've had only a few chance meetings with bears.

Dangerous encounters with bears happen where they have lost their fear of man. A few years ago, while visiting Yellowstone Park with my family, I had a most interesting encounter with a bear. My brother-in-law and I returned to camp one morning after a catching a few trout in Yellowstone Lake. The family wanted to see more of the park, so we decided to take the fish with us and stop later at a picnic area for a fish fry.

We found a site near the river and set up the camp stove on the table. Leaving my wife and the kids to fry the fish, I went down to the river to scour a blackened pot with sand and running water. Out of the quiet morning came screams from the children, "Its a bear!" Running up the bank I saw a large black bear, trotting across the road, nose in the air, sniffing his way toward the frying fish.

Confident in my experience with bears and knowing that park rangers chased away bears all the time in Yellowstone, I stepped in front of the table, hollering and waving my arms. Then I ran directly at the bear. The bear stopped, turned around, and ran back in the direction it came from.

Proudly I explained to my brother-in -law, "Bears don't like humans and are afraid of human intervention." As my wife and children watched through the windows of our locked car, I calmly turned the frying fish and set the table while chuckling to myself. Soon everyone came out of the vehicle, and we sat down for a lovely lunch. About then I glanced across the road, and all followed my stare at the bear who was coming at us— this time on a dead run.

Now I was mad. Brandishing the frying pan, I placed myself in front of the table and again yelled at the bear. My brother-in-law, having great faith in my outdoor skills, stood right behind me. The rest of the family ran for the car. The bear stopped at a range too close for anyone's comfort, but I looked him in the eye. The eyes of a bear are not pleasant. Pig's eyes, though small like a bear's, are full of intelligent interest and friendly curiosity. The eyes of a bear are totally devoid of feeling.

At the moment our gazes locked I did not like what I saw at all. The next instant the bear was clawing clumps of sod and tossing dirt in the air. Then he charged. The speed he could move was unbelievable. Not even having a split second to decide to move, I just stood there. The bear skidded to a halt within arm's reach. Instead of rearing up, crushing my ribs and biting my face off, he calmly turned and walked away.

Dropping to my knees, nerves shattered, I still couldn't move two feet back to the table. Brother-in-law from somewhere back there asked, "Was he bluffing?"

I regained my composure as we loaded our gear in the car. We drove off within minutes and looking back saw the bear again loping across the road for the picnic table.

Another Bear

My other major memory of bear encounters happened in Canada. Most of my bear experiences have been sightings when riding or hiking in the backcountry, but this time I learned two lessons. Ken, a cousin, and I planned a fishing trip in the bush early one summer. Since we had read extensively about the area prior to the trip, we knew of an old logging operation on a river famed for fish and which was far into the backcountry. We would have to portage the boat and pick up the trail that should lead to the river and former logging camp.

Canadian fishing in 1965.

We made it to the river where we found slabs cut off the ends of logs with brands on them. I told Ken how years ago unscrupulous loggers had snagged logs out of the river, cut the branded ends off, and added their company's brand to the log, which they would then send back down the river to the mill. Many companies floated logs down the river to the same mill, so it was not too hard to set up an unlawful operation.

A couple hours hike brought us to the old logging camp. There was one cabin that still had a decent roof and a garbage can hanging about ten feet above the floor from the roof beam. The only window, which was next to the door, had been smashed out and a couple boards were nailed across a piece of cardboard that covered the hole. A note on it read, "The bear came back—broke in again—John."

A light drizzle had started, but we decided to fish an upper pond for speckled (brook) trout. We were soon wet and cold, so I decided to go back to the cabin and start a fire so that when Ken came back we could get dry and warm.

Slogging back to the cabin I kept thinking about that bear. Inside the cabin I found some wood by the fireplace and began splitting kindling. I was on my hands and knees starting the fire when I heard a low grunting growl. With teeth chattering, I turned and looked at the large gap under the door. Something with reddish brown hair was moving toward the window!

My heart almost jumped out of my throat and my mind raced, "that bear is coming through the window!" I stood poised at the door, ready to dash out when the bear would be in the window. Timing was everything. I stood there planning the quick escape. I did not have a gun; I never carried one with me when fishing in all my years in the outdoors—I always thought it could get me into more trouble than it would get me out of. But I still had the hatchet in hand when the door started to creak open. I went for the window, splintering boards and slashing cardboard. I must have landed on my feet because I was instantly at a dead run. When I looked back, there was Ken, doubled up, holding his sides, gales of laughter twisting his face.

It seems that his pretense of bear sounds that were meant to scare me coincided, as he approached, with a marmot scuttling along the bottom of the cabin doorway. Good thing I didn't have a gun; I might have shot him.

What did I learn? The fears that you conjure up in your mind are far scarier than any you face in reality; and, if you are concerned about being in bear country, take along a buddy you can outrun. Then you're safe.

Pierre LeTreque:
An Unguided Tour of the Canadian Back Woods

I have always thought one of the best travel buys in the world is the great outdoors. When alone in nature you make the discoveries; what an advantage over taking a tour. You don't learn much. On a tour bus barreling through the country, with some air-conditioner salesman in the next seat calling out questions to the guide like, "How much you figure them windmills cost?"

For excitement you have a driver leaning on the horn scattering peasants like quail, and crossing himself on the sharp turns. The guide usually takes that moment to point out what a fine driver we have today, and how he would appreciate any little thing you feel like giving him at the end of the trip. You're thinking he should get a suspended sentence and more driving lessons. You might see a lot of country, but you certainly don't feel its moods.

Steeped in this belief, my idea of enjoyable travel and life in the outdoors led me to make a portfolio of activities. Like an architect with a sheaf of plans, or with the care of an investor diversifying his savings, I weighed risks and gains. No sensible person is satisfied with only one pursuit in life, though many see only their own work. My idea was to balance the portfolio, including time and resources for spouse and family. Surely no reasonable God would begrudge a man the enjoyment of the beauty of His gift of nature, if a man didn't spend too much time or money on himself.

For this early adventure (June, 1965) my naive plan was to fish the Canadian backcountry on a very limited budget. A letter to Theriault Air Services, Ltd. of Ontario resulted in some inviting information on good fishing lakes in the territories above Lake Superior. Two friends, Thorton, and Horn, coaching colleagues in the southern Michigan school where I began my career in education, were sold instantly on the idea. We could drive up to the Soo (Sault Ste. Marie) by car, then traverse from lake to river to lake by boat until we arrived at good fishing.

This trip was on a very limited budget; we would do it entirely on our own, no hired assistance. Among the three friends, we decided we could scrounge up all the equipment needed-except for a boat large enough for the big waters.

Pondering our options, someone remembered hearing that the band teacher's father-in-law had a boat—big but trailerable. Bob, the band teacher, was not known as an outdoorsman, but our resources were limited; so we talked about the great fishing adventure to Bob. Sure, he would come with us, if we had a big enough boat.

Enthusiastically, he announced that his father-in-law had just the boat. Wow! With the major problem solved, we laid elaborate plans to assault the Canadian bush in search of adventure.

We departed on a Monday morning, traveling north on Highway 131 to the Straits of Mackinaw, and then Queen's Road 17 along the east side of Lake Superior to Wawa, Ontario-east of Thunder Bay. The area is not a wilderness like, say

Camp at Dog Lake.

Northern Ontario between Hearst and Longlac, but it's a lonely region of rolling green hills that gives you an eerie feeling when the gas gauge is low, like somebody who won't quit grinning at you. Fur traders in canoes traversed the province of Ontario, which is shaped like a giant leaping fish, its tail in the lower Great Lakes and back along Hudson Bay, along its 1500 miles for two centuries. We were bound for the belly of the fish.

It's a land of changing seasons and many climates. Climates differ with distance from place to place, I realize; but this area's weather changes from hour to hour. The day began with cool and gusty winds and sudden showers. From Wawa, we went north to Hawk Junction where we launched the boat and began navigating the chain of lakes and rivers.

We packed all our gear in the boat and the four of us gazed out across Hawk Lake, looking for the railroad trestle traversing the north end of the lake. We would have to go under, and it looked pretty low. By bending down we just fit under—the windshield clearing by two inches. After the trestle we followed Hawk River to the Manitowik Lake and river system, dodging snags and floating logs, until we reached Dog Lake where we made camp on the north (windward) side of a small island. We hoped the breeze would keep the mosquitoes and black flies off. The lakeshore was untenable, as the insects found innovative ways to invade every part of our anatomy.

We sat with Bob in the smoke of the campfire and tried to educate him in the woodsman's way of surviving flying "biters." Mosquitoes are attracted not only by sweat but also exhaled carbon dioxide, we told him. "Your breath is the activator of host-seeking behavior, stimulating them to bite. Keep your mouth closed, and if you must breathe then go sit by yourself over there."

From the island we fished for Walleye, Lake Trout and Pike with moderate success. By the third day we were running low on bread and beer, so Bob and I volunteered to go back to Hawk Junction for supplies.

Early on day four we headed back across Dog Lake toward civilization with the big 50 horse Mercury flying the boat low over the water. Loons, drifting in pairs, dived for cover as we roared by. Bob was having the time of his life, so I taught him a song to go with his Canadian fantasy. Bob was standing, driving the boat, wind in his hair, singing:

"I'm Pierre LeTreque, de man of de North,
I hunt de bear, I hunt de wolf..."

I tried to point out to "Pierre" the floating logs and snags in the lake, remnants of lumbering days; but as we swerved our way through the river system he continued full throttle, singing all the way. Finally, I grabbed his arm and tried to reason with him. We had barely made it under the railroad trestle, fully loaded with four people in the boat; he had better slow down!

"We made it in; we'll make it out," he yelled. Around the last bend we flew, heading straight into the water swirling under the trestle. As we approached, I could see very little light under the opening from the other side.

I started yelling, "We're not going to make it under!"

He kept hollering, "Yes, we will." About thirty yards from the opening he screamed, "We're not going to make it!" and reared back on the throttle. We hit the floor, and the wake caught us and slammed the boat under the trestle smashing the windshield level with the fore deck. With a horrible screech of fiberglass against creosoted timber we ground to a stop, wedged about twenty feet into the opening. The bow was wedged under a beam; there were only a couple inches between the gunnel and the ties; and the transom was cocked up just outside the outer beam.

The gang!

Not what you would call real success but he caught a fish.

I looked at Bob, took out my hunting knife, and said, "I'm cutting a hole in the floor of the boat and sinking it. We're getting out of here."

He protested that we at least ought to try to flip

over on our backs and push with our feet against the ties above us. We only managed to bob up and down; the boat would not move.

Bob started hollering for help, and I tried to calm him by considering the possibilities. "There are probably two people a year who go this far into the bush. Since we have all summer, we went in and we came out, so what do you think our chances are of someone coming along."

I tried to keep my sense of humor, a vital part of my outdoor survival equipment, but I was not laughing. I was stuck under a railroad trestle with a raving "Pierre." We probably spent half an hour with Bob screaming 'til his lungs gave out. Then as I listened to the blessed silence, the faint drone of a motorboat drifted across the lake. As it came nearer the trestle we both started hollering.

The motor stopped, and we heard splashing as a man swam up to the transom of our boat. "How long you been stuck in there?" he hollered.

Without much thought, I replied, "A week!"

We couldn't see him, caught as we were under the dark trestle, but we heard him say, "Oh my God," and he splashed away.

A few minutes later he was back, and over the gunnel two packs of crackers and a Snicker bar dropped into the boat. I felt a little guilty, telling him we'd been here a week, but it seemed that long with a bellowing Pierre beside me in close quarters.

Fishing buddies

Our rescuer said he had a ski rope, and he and his friend would try to pull us out. The smaller boat went under the trestle and tied onto our bow. As we assumed the position in the bottom of the boat, pushing with our feet on the trestle beams, the swimmer pushed and rocked as best he could. Moving little by little, we worked the boat out from under the ties and into the lake beyond.

We thanked them effusively, admitting we hadn't been stuck for quite a week, but never saying exactly how long.

We continued very slowly along the shore to Hawk Junction, and tried to put things into perspective. How were we going to get back with supplies to our buddies in the bush? As we went about gathering supplies the locals enlightened us about *the hydroelectric dam* on the river, which caused drastic fluctuations in water level of the lake. We could wait two days, and the lake would be lower. The good news was we could fish

Back from a fishing trip in Canada, 1961, my wife, Carolyn and myself.

Hawk Lake; the bad news: we had to sleep in the boat with only our jackets for warmth. "Hey, Pierre, we having fun yet?"

Two days passed, and we cleared the trestle opening and went to fetch the boys in the backcountry. They gave us a lot of flack, accusing us of spending two days drinking beer and

Canadian trip, 1965.

chasing women. I protested that my family, which I dearly love, only allowed me to be a *man's man,* not a *ladies man.* I had released enough testosterone in the socially accepted manner, solving problems in the wild. That quieted them down.

Bob was plenty quiet for the whole trip home, rehearsing in his mind, I guess, what he'd tell his father-in-law about the boat. Sometimes going home is the best part of the trip.

Sheba

"Any veteran of the mountains," they say "cares for his horse and then for himself." I hope I've always done this.

In the mid-1600s the Utes acquired "magic dogs" (commonly known as horses) from the Spanish. This led to a drastic lifestyle change and a love affair between horses and mountain folks ever since. Just like you and your favorite dog, horse owners have one horse they will never forget. That horse for me was Sheba, a partner to whom I owe a large debt of gratitude, and a horse that deserves this tribute.

In 1972 I purchased a horse from an old outfitter who had bred a Welsh pony to an Appaloosa, to get a hardy, black hoofed (holds the shoe better, tougher feet), compact horse, with big lungs, for mountain use. The result was Sheba, a year and a half old and only "green broke."

At the time she didn't have a name, being wild and woolly and apt to give you the last ride of your life, unless you could prove you were not coming off. Many a time I thought she should go to the glue factory; but my father kept telling me, "break the horse not her spirit." As we called all the horses in our pack train until they earned a name for themselves, she was "shit head"—in her case, for the next two years.

She had been taken to the high country since she was six months old, and once on a mountain trail, she would settle in and do fine—though, a pleasure rider she was not. Most horses

Sheba, grazing at camp in the mountains.

steer fairly easily and have several forward speeds. One is a jog that jars your molars, another is the lope that rattles the whole skeleton and avoids their full trot because "trots" is a nasty word. She walked as well as a Tennessee Walker, rode as easily as a mule, had the durability of a quarter horse, and was smart as a donkey. She was the horse we put the novice or the city slicker on for their first trip to the mountains. Over the years Sheba became the perfect horse for our use.

Many times I rode her over the Continental Divide at night, in the pitch dark, for the three and a half hours to our

Sheba and me, trying to find a camp.

camp. She would follow a sheep trail at times, as much off as on the trail. Occasionally I would try to pull her back on the trail; but when she would insist on turning, I'd pull out my light and sure enough the sheep trail would break off, and she would lead us around a willow bog— the only way to avoid a tangled mess. Over the years I learned to let her go, and she would take me wherever I wanted. How she knew the way, I'll never comprehend. Animals use their senses in ways we have yet to understand. Just thinking about this extraordinary animal lifts my respect nearly to awe.

It's not that they are more intelligent than other animals or humans. Horses recognize some loud sounds, such as the voice of the right person with a voice of authority, and they trust a command to cross a noisy rushing stream in a rocky bed. Though horses are frightened by unfamiliar sounds, like the hollow echo of hooves on a footbridge which give them the feeling it's not safe, they may trust their rider's order to go ahead. Or they may believe the rider who tells them with voice or legs that the soft bog or muddy path is not quicksand; but he better be right, or that horse will need to be trained all over again.

We trained Sheba through her belly, because it was larger than her brain. In camp I could untie her, and she would graze, unhobbled, until it was time for her desert, a molasses and grain "biscuit." She must have been addicted to those cubes, because she would come anytime from anywhere if she heard two cubes clicked together. She was easy to tie up, and never too far away, always with an ear out for a biscuit.

She became a good friend on long, lonely trips. I would talk to her like a person; she'd just roll those big brown eyes. So it's easy to understand the attachment mountain men had for their horses. I've heard of starving men not able to eat their horse, but instead drinking its blood for nourishment. The reasoning was, the horse could replenish its blood by grazing.

Packing in with Sheba's colt.

There were times I was hungry enough to think about the possibility, but I couldn't bring myself to do it.

The pecking order in our string of horses became well established early in Sheba's career; she dominated all the other horses regardless of their size. She was the lead horse and would eat first, which was only fair because she faced the risks of the trail first. One time, during a long ride of about eight hours, we came up on a shepherd grazing his flock across a glacier carved valley. Off the hill charged his dog. From the horse behind came a snort and a head toss that translated, "That dog is going to eat us alive!"

"No," I explained, "that's not a dog baring his teeth to scare you; he's just smiling." Up the rise the dog stormed, snap-

Sheba at home for a rest.

ping and snarling. "You better look out, Sheba." She just turned her head and rolled her eyes, watching the dog at her heels. When he came in close enough, she flicked out a hoof and caught the dog full in the side without ever missing her stride. The dog rolled, end over end, down the hill and ran yelping up his side of the valley. I hope she didn't break any ribs or hurt him too much.

Caught out in a snowstorm one time, I took shelter in a mining ghost town. I tried to bring her into an old shed where mules had been kept, but she would not come. Then I realized she had never been inside a building in her life. She was born outside, lived in a field, roamed the Colorado mountains, and had never been under a barn roof, ever! I sat in the shed watching her standing out in the weather, snow drifting around her where she had turned her butt to the wind. Munching oats in her nosebag, she seemed plenty comfortable.

Sheba could be packed, ridden, or even pull a hiker up the slope with her tail and never get excited. This horse would thread her way down a descent so precipitous that looking down, I could see ground falling away beneath her feet; but she never fell with a rider. At night, she would skirt the trees on the trail, not rubbing the pack or your knees. She seemed to know the danger in night riding of running a stub of spruce or pine through your eye.

When we worked clearing forest service trails, Sheba was the horse to pack logs on, one on each side, hauling them up the mountain to build water diversions or foot bridges over boggy areas. Sometimes she couldn't move her head from side to side because of the length of the logs, but she just plodded on up the mountain. We tended to give her heavier packs over the years, until the time she slid all the way down a mountainside backwards, because she didn't have traction in the snow. As I ran down the mountain after her I could see those big brown eyes rolling white, and I just kept yelling, "It's OK Sheba, hang still." She never floundered about, and when I got to her she

Pleasure riding with Sheba.

held still until I could cut the cinches and repack. Then away we went again.

After the time she brought a boy and me through the blizzard whiteout ("Survival Elk Hunt") I told my wife, " When Sheba goes, I quit!" But, I lied. She carried on and retired after twenty-five years of working the trails. We lost her in 1998 at twenty-seven and a half years old, and I'm not ashamed to say I cried.

The Cliff Hanger

On this particular hunt we were heading back into the country where the Rio Grande has its beginning, a place we call the "Enchanted Forest." The remarkable thing about this area was not the beautiful alpine meadows surrounding the big trees. Even the extraordinary sightings of wildlife did not define the special character of the place. The trees themselves made this location so dramatic—dimly lit hallways of stark mossy pillars, a forest of Engleman Spruce. This was perfect elk habitat, because it had the cover, the food, and the marshy spots they seek.

We left camp half an hour before dawn, four of us: two hunters and two guides. The plan was to set the hunters up on the northern edge of the timber, since early in the morning elk are usually feeding on the lush grasses of the meadow that dropped sharply to a valley below. After placing the hunters in position, the other guide and I would circle the woods in opposite directions. We would stay close to the timber and perhaps spot elk returning from other meadows.

My horse, Sheba, picked our way along the edge of the forest as early light broke through the trees, shredding the mist that drifted down from the peaks. Deadfalls were everywhere, each with a sassy little squirrel chirping questions I could have answered with a hundred and thirty grain statement, but it was their home—I the invader. Besides, I never carry a gun when I'm the outfitter.

A loose system of trails penetrates this backcountry, and a horse will follow them if you don't direct them otherwise. I have to have a good horse, because my mind is always wandering and absorbing. At that time I was watching the procession of clouds rolling over a saddle on the skyline of sharply cut ridges above the timber. You have to keep a weather eye out, because summer and winter can come on the same day, usually two hours of summer and twenty-two hours of winter. Morning sunlight streaked across the eastern sky and bathed the meadows in a reddish glow. With a whisper in the spruce, a cold wind came biting into my face. No wonder folks out west who spend much time outdoors have wrinkled faces. I tell people these aren't crow's feet, they're laugh lines—so I 'm still pretty. I looked around at the browse (plants that took years to grow and produce seeds) and the elk have come along and nipped them off, leaving only a stem. It doesn't seem fair when you consider the food chain and cycle of life.

If you are quiet it's amazing how little you disturb nature and how much the wilderness will reveal as you ride along. Some folks feel they were in the wilderness after they've driven down a road with forest on both sides. I think the wilderness starts two days from the nearest trailhead.

Suddenly the crack of a rifle brought me back to the reason we were here. The sound came from back where we left the two hunters. Not being in a hurry (the elk either drops or you let him go and wait twenty minutes) I continued around the

"Enchanted Forest." Then another shot, coming from the same direction, broke the stillness of the morning. Moving on around the woods, I still had not met my partner. As I crested a small rise I spotted one of the hunters lying in the open on the side of a hill.

An hour had passed since I heard the first shot. Riding up to the man, who appeared to be sleeping, I noticed blood on his face and hands. "Oh, my God," I thought, "he's been shot." I dismounted and ran over to him in a panic. Slowly, he sat up, looked at me and lay back down. Gingerly I touched his arm and asked him if he were okay.

"I'm dead," was his only response.

This was one of those moments when you realize there can be hell on earth. My experiences in the fascinating outdoor world are filled with exciting episodes, but this one I had hoped to avoid.

While I stood meditating over him, someone came from behind and clutched my arm. I jumped, instantly swinging and kicking. My nerves were fast unraveling. The other hunter, now safely out of my space, hollered "Calm down. Are you crazy?"

My reply was, "Yes, I'm headed that direction!"

They related their story. They had been sitting on the edge of the timber where we left them and had watched the meadow below. Placing their rifles on their daypacks beside them, they waited for enough light for shooting. In the stillness they began to hear the sounds: grunting, chomping, and the swish of steps in the vegetation. They strained through binoculars to see the elk making these sounds in the dim light and heavy mist. Out of the haze a five point bull appeared, not thirty yards in front of them. The presence of game in such close proximity is exciting and scary at the same time. The fear is of making a mistake.

The injured hunter told how he slowly leaned down to peer through the scope of his rifle with as little motion as possible, so as to focus on the elk. His friend had said shoot and having the elk in the scope, he pulled the trigger. "Pow!" A circle was cut around his eye by the recoil of the rifle just lying on the pack, not snugged up to his shoulder. The other hunter, watching the bull just stand there, whispered, "Wait, I think he's hit." Time passes slowly in these moments. Then, "Shoot," the command came again. Leaning over, sighting through the scope, this time pulling his eye back from it, he fired. "Pow!" One deep circle cut around his nose.

Instead of going down, the bull charged to the left of the hunters, crashed into the timber and disappeared. Both hunters jumped up and chased the elk into the woods. At elevations of 12,000 feet you don't outrun an elk, wounded or not. The snow from an early storm remained in the shade of the forest, so they followed the easy trail at a run. They figured the elk was headed for open country on the other side, and they could get another shot in the clear. Coming to the hillside where I found them, the elk was nowhere to be seen, and they had collapsed, feeling like grim death from lack of oxygen.

This episode was not over; it was just beginning for me and my buddy, who had just showed up. We took the walking dead down to a creek, washed the one up, and put them on the horses. Telling them that we'd try to track the elk while they went back to camp, we watched as they went through the creek, up the other side, and disappeared behind a ridge. Reappearing on the next knoll was one horse and rider and one horse with an empty saddle. Off we went running now over the ridge, where we spotted our battered bloody hunter lying on the ground. Before we could get to him, he rolled over, got up and seeing us gave the "go to hell" wave and started in the direction of camp.

All right, let's get back to business. Up in the snow where the elk came out of the timber we picked up the trail, but even searching on hands and knees we found no sign of blood or hair. The tracks headed downhill, a good sign, but eventually mixed with a thousand others, old and new.

Savages were more skillful at tracking than civilized folk, because tracking was their serious life-long pursuit. For me the ideal time for tracking is when the ground is white. After the first snow the primal stalking instincts seem to materialize from out of nowhere. I kept thinking, "all living creatures have peculiarities, and all of these marks and behaviors make a singular trail. It begins at the birthplace of that creature and ends with its death. So why can't I find and follow it when I want?" Maybe I've injured my eyes reading too many books.

Placing a hat at the last known track of this elk, we worked our way down to the creek, now occasionally finding a blood spot. There was one in the snow the size of a baseball, then nothing. We studied the terrain, examining the probabilities of which way he would go. If south, the creek formed a huge canyon, and as it looped east made a barrier that could not be traversed either down or across, unless you had wings. We had crawled around four and a half hours trying to unravel the track. I recalled doing this for twenty-one hours one time, the thought of which was making me sick. In my mind the comfort of our guests is always first, so we decided to head back to camp and check the hunters.

We made a beeline toward the canyon and soon were walking along the rim planning to work eastward to camp. Then we spotted a five point bull hunkered down on a precipice extending from the rim of the canyon. The elk had walked out along a ridge no more than a foot wide, and was now looking down on a drop of 400 feet on either side. The bull just sat there, evidently mortally wounded, or he would not have made that critical mistake. We decided to have me guard the ridge, so he couldn't come back; and my partner would go back to camp and bring the hunter back with his rifle. Off he ran leaving me there with a rock in my hand. The things that go through a man's mind in such a position, I will not attempt to explain. If the bull had decided to make the return trip I guess I was supposed to conk him with the rock and hang on.

It seemed like three hours later (twenty minutes they claimed) when the group came running back. We got the

The cliff-hanging elk.

hunter in position, and he did the humane act of putting the animal out of his misery. Now how did we get him back off the narrow ridge?

Great minds look for easy solutions to simple problems; sometimes they don't exist. The thought in my mind was, "with one million hunters, after Rocky Mountain elk, in nine western states, how did I end up in this situation?" I heaved a sigh and

The elk out on the ledge.

told the other guide that we better go out on the ledge, draw and quarter the elk, and haul the quarters back one at a time. We instructed the hunters to sit tight and not go out on the ledge since we didn't want them to fall to their death on our watch. We did worry about leaving them alone to be eaten by bear or field mice, but we took our chances.

The wind picked up about then, driving a cold that was not just a knife, but also a bludgeon beating on us. Behind the wind came rain, making the ledge slippery at a rate you couldn't believe. With no further discussion I climbed carefully out to where the bull was balancing and kicked it off the ledge toward the river some 400 feet below.

My heart pounded in my chest as I watched the elk tumble down the rocky cliff, dehorned and tenderized by the time it hit bottom. Then I had only to inch my way back off the ridge without slipping and adding my carcass to the one below. The trip back was focused and fascinating but uneventful. I think it takes a special talent to be able to switch your brain on and off at will.

After working the horses up from our camp a mile downstream to the elk, we finished field dressing it and packed the quarters back. With the proud hunter in camp, his first elk hunt a success, it all seemed worthwhile. In retrospect, these were two of the very best people to enjoy an outing with. I enjoyed their outlook on life and their respect shown to others. I hope to look them up in my travels some day. They are my kind of people. The "Enchanted Forest" appeared to still hold its charm for a special hunt and magnificent elk. Thank you for another great outdoor experience.

The Tracker

The outfitting trips I enjoy the most are spontaneous. It's the same principle with sex, though that's not my topic. I am talking about doing the things you enjoy when you want to.

It was a bright morning, August 20, 1981, when I called my buddy, Jerry, and encouraged him to ride with me and set up a bow camp for the upcoming Colorado archery season. He agreed, so we loaded horses in the trailer and set out for Silverton from my ranch south of Montrose along Highway 550 toward Ouray.

Putting shoes on the horses, getting them ready to go.

The approach to Silverton is dramatic whether you come from the north across the Million Dollar Highway from Ouray and descend from the 11,018-foot crest of Red Mountain Pass, or drive up from the south across Molas Divide. From the latter the highway zigzags down to Baker Park where Silverton, looking like a toy village, appears at the west end of the flat park, dwarfed by the mountains that surround it. Threads of roads fan out from Silverton and twist up gulches filled with mineral deposits.

The Brunot Treaty with the Utes, which was signed in 1873, opened this area to prospectors. They looked feverishly for gold but found mostly silver. By 1875 the whole region was alive with men, and new camps were burgeoning near the most productive claims. Many remnants of these bygone years still persist.

Otto Mears, the road builder of the San Juan Range, hewed a toll road from the solid rock walls hundreds of feet above the Uncompahgre River. His vision and achievement made possible the present Million Dollar Highway that connects Ouray to Silverton.

Upon arriving at Silverton we went north to Maggie Gulch where we unloaded the horses and packed them for the ride to an old mine up at the high end of Maggie.

Cool days precede increasingly colder nights as late autumn moves into the mountains. Aspens become flames of color before their leaves are torn loose and swirled away by the wind. Beneath the trees the forest growth thins, revealing glacial rocks and fallen logs. The unique autumn smells permeate every gully, ridge, and meadow. Elk begin to move from the timber into the parks for fall grazing. The peaks have received their first touch of snow, and the year's growth is over.

Our destination was over the Continental Divide traversing from west to east. Slowly we rode toward the top. "Barren" is the description applied to the treeless tundra of the high ridges. Winter rules this land for nine months of the year. The growing season is sometimes as short as fourteen days. An old pine clings to the rocky precipices near the top of the divide. Some say the bristlecone pines growing at these altitudes are the oldest living things on earth. Guardians of the heights, they inspire a determination to go on, continuing to live as they do, despite all disruptions from the elements. I felt something in the cold damp air against my cheek and shuddered at memories of tougher outings in the mountains.

Working our way along a sheep trail, we descended into a valley formed by West Pole Creek. The deciduous trees were bare of leaf; knowing they must give up their profligate life to be born again in summer, they scatter their foliage in a burst of color. The conservative evergreens live year round. Once in the timber we set up camp in a small park protected by larger spruce.

Before dawn the next morning we had a light breakfast and coffee, the life-blood of a mountain man, cowboy survival fluid. We then started up the mountain side intending to find an elk herd, so we could tell the hunters where they could prob-

A simple camp. I stayed there three days.

ably find elk close enough for a bow shot. The forest is dark and mysterious at this hour—silence prevails. Then dawn comes and rewards the straining eyes with the sight of trees at their greenest and the rocks are luminescent.

The trail moves us up a staircase of rocks. Except for my and my companion's step, there is still only silence. A buddy is someone who can sense your mood and think the same things at the same time without the need for conversation. My wife always wants to know what we talk about. I tell her, "nothing." She doesn't understand that. The trail skirts a ridge, and a light wind cools our brows, tickles our nostrils, and stirs our minds. Here there is space. The mountain weaves upward, blending with sky. The thin air makes our lungs work as they should but with increasing effort; fatigue slowly sets in. Minutes later and a few hundred feet higher I realize our idea of adventure is about to reach the limitation of reality. It has been a long trek already.

My buddy, Jerry, looks like Grizzly Adams, with his full beard and 270 pounds on a 6'-1" frame. I'm 5'-8" at 180, so the climb was taking a greater toll on his energy. Stepping out into a clearing at the timberline, Jerry ducks and whispers, "Elk just over the next ridge." Slowly he crawls up the game trail through the heather with me bobbing along behind.

There was a five-point bull standing on a ledge fifty yards above us. Jerry turned and putting his finger to lips said, "Shish, you can smell them." Bent over, following him up the narrow path through the brush we continued. The closer we got, the lower he crouched, eventually crawling on his stomach. Watching him slithering up the well-used game path, and noting large quantities of the olive-sized pellets of elk droppings along the trail, I knew he must have been smearing himself with shit from his chest to his toes. Jerry, who was staring intently ahead, eyes on the bull as he dragged his body along, was unaware of the situation.

I said, "Can you still smell elk?" but unable to control myself I started chuckling and then laughing until my stomach ached and I was gasping for breath. I pictured telling the hunters about the great prowess of this stalker who could get so close to the elk he could smell them. Laughing hysterically, I slid off the side of the trail. I was laughing so hard the bull ran away, taking probably a hundred head with him in a mad dash to escape the unusual commotion. Rolling up alongside a bolder thirty yards below, still choked with laughter, I managed to holler, "You smell like you got real close to the wild Wapiti."

Jerry realized his vulnerable position in future campfire stories, so he retaliated in his normal Neanderthal behavior. Grabbing the front of my jacket, he swung me around and held my body off a cliff with a drop of some three hundred feet. Screaming he explained the new situation to me, "If you don't scrape all the elk manure off my clothes, I'll throw you off the ledge."

With one toe on rock and the rest of me dangling in air, I balanced and laughed, tears filling my eyes. He, with equally red face set upon vengeance, kept repeating his orders. I explained to him that in no way did he want my hunting knife close to his crotch.

In due time he regained his senses and hauled my body from being suspended in mid-air back to safe ground. I

Grizzle Adams, that's a big horse.

dropped to my knees still laughing at this big man, with a big beard, caught in this big dilemma. Gradually we regained our sobriety and walked back to camp. After that episode things were anticlimactic.

A week later, with the hunters in camp, I tried to tell the story, but he jumped in, defusing the situation by explaining how we both crawled through elk droppings in our attempt to get close to the herd.

Let the man have his pride!

Outfitting

Why would a person with a University Degree (Western Michigan University, 1963) decide to become an outfitter and guide in Colorado?

Part of the answer lies in the year I was born, 1940. It was a time between the darkness of the Great Depression and the storms of World War II, a critical time in shaping the next generation. We were all poised for a better life. Our land was changing from an agrarian to an urban society. No matter how well educated we might be, we were all searching for happiness in the way we live. If we did not find it, we tended to destroy ourselves or those around us.

While growing up, my brother and I didn't wear shoes in the summer so we could have a decent pair in the winter. There were no swimming pools in our little town, so we took our dip in the lakes and rivers. Our world was defined by the square mile around our town, but we knew there was a big world out there.

We trained ourselves so well, we believed nothing could do us harm. As we grew older our lives were shaped by war issues: the Korean police action, the Cold War, and other issues at home: of race and economic opportunity. My family was not victimized by affluence or a lack of it; we appreciated little things, and the children in my family were encouraged to develop a sense of personal responsibility and a commitment to honesty.

Todd Richardson and myself, guiding on a successful bow hunt for Chuck Davis.

Another belief we held was that hunting and fishing were the common man's recreation. What better calling could there be than making a living doing what you loved? Imagine, having fun and getting paid for it! I don't think anyone departs very far from who they were in early life. Pleasure is seldom found in working, phooey! Pleasure is found in leisure. I wanted to share my interest in the outdoors, to help people appreciate and enjoy the good things, and to get high on the wild!

With this background I became an outfitter, and the realities soon became apparent. My buddy called outfitting "a three month hell of worry and toil." For him it was an accurate description, but there is for many of us an eternal romance with nature, that will not fade away in the light of toil and responsibility.

After spending thirty years in the mountains I have not changed. The biggest day of the year is still that day when I wake up stretched out on the ground, frost covering the tarp over my sleeping bag (rated -40°), and I begin to see the light creeping over the mountains. They are like white feathered war bonnets over the rim of the world.

Hunting expeditions are written up by the thousands, but few write of the kind that you and I go on. What are the possibilities of ordinary folks enjoying the beauty and adventure of mountain hunting without paying big money for a private hunt on a big private ranch? The pleasure, benefit, advantage, and the real glory of the outfitter appears destined for oblivion as this country changes in its economic diversity, and hunters change in their expectations. One can now hunt in a fenced-in game ranch with a guaranteed kill. But, oh, what is lost in the process.

In our outfitting management, we don't rifle hunt on our bow hunting area, a 5,600-acre permit at 11,000 ft. We also don't bow hunt on our rifle area, 10,000 acres at 10,400 ft. And we don't outfit for just any head and hide, though we have no

The first bull.

problem if others do. We concentrate on elk and deer since they are doing well in Colorado. We have more elk now than anytime in the history of the state.

I was asked by one man how one gets to be an outfitter. I told him, "Stick with your normal job until you're forty, then you're not fit for anything else have a guardian angel (one probably won't be enough, better get a whole squad of 'em) and they'll all be over-worked!"

Constantly I used to reassure my wife, "My life insurance is paid up, don't worry." The last time I used that line, she replied, "Insurance is to replace the item with exactly the one that's been destroyed."

"If that's the way it is, cancel the policy before it's too late!" I never used that line again.

Let's think about you, the hunter, and me the outfitter. Watch the outfitter you choose; he can punish you. Many develop a "no bullshit" attitude, never wanting to show a nice side to their personality. You may hear them say, " Do you want to walk out of here?" Or one degree softer, "Do you want to ride that

*One of the great thrills of my life was to have my son, "Randy,"
enjoy the outdoors with me. I am on the right, Randy is in the
middle.*

horse out alone?" How about, "If you don't like heights, look the
other way." Make sure he loves you, and it's not just doctor's
bedside manner. Remember, even though you hired him as a
beast of burden, you are subordinate; you cannot function
without that man's help. Try to understand your outfitter is a
businessman, with costs for liability, permits, vehicles, labor,
leases, equipment, and travel. Even though he functions as a
beast of burden he may resent it a little. A healthy sense of

Bow hunters are a wonderful group to outfit as they like to hunt and usually work hard at it.

humor is often the best solution to many difficult situations. Without an ability to laugh at troubles and hard times, nobody can truly enjoy the outdoors, especially as an outfitter.

You can sometimes judge an outfitter's sense of humor from his slang. Does he call the cook a *beanmaster* who puts *axelgrease* on the *hot rocks* and expects you to sink your *nut-crackers* into 'em (teeth into buttered biscuits)? Does he see the dishwasher as *a pearl diver*, and *rollin' the cotton* as breaking camp? If he says "Easy with them *rib wrenches*, or you'll be *ridin' the long trail*," it's just his genteel way of saying, "Use less spurs or that horse might be the death of you."

Your outfitter should be established and knowledgeable. Much of our information on deer and elk seasonal habitat is gleaned from visits with sheepherders who spend the summer in the highest backcountry. They will run up to 3,000 sheep in a single herd, the maximum one man with dogs can handle. The shepherd's life is a hard one. The wonder, I say, is not that some go crazy, but that any of them stay sane. We bring them hard candy, like lemon drops and butterscotch, and they explain where the elk were, their numbers, sex and ages throughout the three months they are in the high country. When they say "mucho elk" it is very reliable information.

Another good source is Forest Service workers who clean the mountain trails in the summer. They will indicate on our maps where they have seen the deer and elk. In return we let them stay in our cabins scattered through the mountains, which is especially appreciated in bad weather.

Different outfitters have various preferences for packing animals and what animals to pack. The first consideration in loading is balance. The various bundles are cinched with knots and hitches designed for quick release, in case the animal stum-

*Todd and I
guiding out
of the cabin.*

bles in the brush. A mule can carry as much as a hundred pounds in each side pannier, but I try to keep it down to seventy-five. For just packing, there is no comparison between a mule and a horse; a mule will carry heavier loads, easier and farther on less food, and it is more sure-footed. A mule will step off the trail or go around a tree to avoid knocking a pack off, while a horse will bump and bang panniers constantly. However, mules are stubborn.

There is a new breed of high country pack animal seen more every season, the llama. They will willingly carry from sixty to eighty pounds, but exceed their own personally prescribed limit, and they simply sit down. Highly intelligent, easily trained, and possessed of a childlike curiosity, llamas make pleasant trail companions. Another consideration is that unlike horses, a llama's soft padded feet make very little impact on delicate wilderness trails. But, llamas cannot carry a person out of

A nice bull, getting ready to haul him out.

the backcountry in case of an emergency.

My favorite, as you have by now gathered, is the horse. You can pack, ride, haul, and enjoy them through many situations. You can haul your equipment and supplies in, and your game or buddy's body off the mountain, if need be. There's no perfect animal, just as there's no perfect vehicle for all occasions. Each one works in their own way for different people and purposes.

You may go to the wilderness with an outfitter-guide, or go on your own, but keep in mind that nature has its own way of maintaining balance in the outdoorsman population. When you go on your own and you mess up, if you make it back, you can just deny you ever tried. People ask me, "Have you survived an earthquake, a tornado?" I tell them, "No, but I have survived forty-five hunting seasons!"

You Don't Win Them All

I find it easy to send my mind the places, but it's so hard for my body to follow.

In 1970 I purchased a gold mine in the mountains outside Silverton, Colorado. It was a ten-acre claim purchased from a person who had bought it for back taxes. *Durant No. 2*, located at 11,400 feet, was a lovely plot of land with a small creek running through the property, and it was situated on the trailhead entering the Weminuche Wilderness area. My dream was to eventually have a cabin on the land surrounded by thousands of acres of public land in the San Juan National Forest.

Not being totally foolish, I sent to the Department of the Interior for a survey description of the claim and received the original survey notes dating back to 1902. The tract lay 1,565 feet N by NW from the corner marker of Deer Park. Armed with this information I crudely surveyed it, and all seemed perfect. The claim had produced gold and silver through a one-man operation for quite some time.

We used the ten acres for a hunting camp and summer tent camping expeditions into the wilderness. Nothing much was done with it through the next ten years. The 1980s saw the price of gold climb to a record eight hundred dollars an ounce. Now was the time to experiment!

As I read all I could find on one-man gold mining operations, a plan began developing. I would build a sluice box to

Looking over our beloved mining claim.

divert the stream, go into the mine thirty feet into the bedrock, sweep the floor, and pick up all the gold that had been working through the faults for the last eighty years. The plan perfected, I spent many days that summer working the stream, diverting the creek and digging beneath little drops where the gold would collect.

Working hardrock with my son.

By the end of the summer forty pounds of blue clay with good "color" had been accumulated. A local mining veteran viewed the color and advised me to go for it. The sluice box floor was matted with burlap, so the gold would work in to the weave as the water and debris washed over it. At summer's end I burned the burlap and saved all the color extracted from it.

Working a sluice box for gold.

During the winter I washed all the color out of the slack and worked it with a gold pan. The next step was to purchase a hundred dollar's worth of mercury. Mercury will pick up its own weight in gold from a pan. Working with tweezers and mercury, I picked up all the color I could and was ready to retort the remainder from the mercury amalgam. The old time process required splitting a potato, hollowing the center, placing mercury in the hollow, then wiring the potato back together. When the potato is heated the mercury will flow into the flesh of the potato, but the gold will remain centered as a nugget, since it will not flow at the relatively low temperature that vaporizes mercury.

With this theory in mind I retorted two potatoes using a propane stove placed out in the middle of a ten-acre field. I stood fifty yards back to avoid the deadly poisonous mercury vapor. When they were well baked I ran out and found, centered in my experiment, two nuggets the size of golf balls. Wow!

The nuggets were sent to California to have them tested for purity. After a week of waiting I got the call. "Very interesting, come on in." The nuggets were pure, pure copper, worth about two and a half cents apiece. One of them I relocated, as far as I could throw it, in the middle of a ten-acre field. The other I kept for posterity.

I told my wife, "I'm going to get some value out of that property yet." I've always thought, "It's OK to fail, but not to quit." I had owned the land for more than ten years and dreamed everyman's dream of a cabin in the wilderness, surrounded by nature. So, the next adventure was to build a cabin on the property.

In the winter months, after teaching school, I would go to my shop and cut floor joists and rafters. I made window and door frames. Horseshoes were bent to make handles—everything was natural and rustic.

Spring arrived and it was time to cut standing dead timber for walls. All the materials were to be on the spot when building started. It was time to carry ninety-pound bags of cement up the mountain where no road led. Logs were snaked to the spot with chains using only manpower, since the terrain was too rough for horses to move logs or even the metal roofing.

Fortunately I had the help of some of my buddies, Jerry Perkins, Don Engburg, and Jerry Reynolds. The idea was that we would all use the cabin for years to come. So in early summer we started the building process. Work was slow; mortaring the foundation and laying the logs was backbreaking labor, but eventually the little cabin began taking shape.

One afternoon when we were about three quarters finished (the doors and windows were set in place) a neighbor came along with his wife and small daughter. He asked us which claim we owned, and what our plans were. They owned a cabin about half a mile away and were excited about having neighbors. We could keep an eye on each other's places.

They invited us to come over for supper, but we protested we were too dirty and sweaty and didn't want to intrude on the family at this time.

"Supper will be ready at 6:30 p.m. Be there!" he announced. We thanked him and went back to work. Later that afternoon we cleaned up as best we could and proceeded down to his cabin.

After a fine meal, which his wife prepared, he laid out his maps and explained that when he built his place, the Bureau of Land Management accused him of taking an old cabin off their property. He protested it was on his land. To settle the dispute the government agency surveyed the land and placed survey markings to attest to the meets and bounds of his property. It is difficult to find the correct boundaries because of the improbability of finding a government corner section marker as this land lies in broken slopes in the middle of nowhere.

With his knowledge of the correct survey markers he explained that in 1902 there was a tract known as Deer Park. Unknown to us, another Lower Deer Park was designated some years later. We were taking our bearings from the marker of Lower Deer Park, but the original meets and bounds referred to the Deer Park above. We were on the wrong claim for Durant No. 2.

The person who sold us the land had made the mistake, and we continued in the same error. The land was purchased through a real estate company, but there was a ten-year limit on protesting the sale. A check of the courthouse records showed the owner of the land we were building on was living in California; our property was another half mile up the mountain.

The terrain made it impossible to drag logs and material further up the mountain. The snows in winter exceeded ten feet up there and came earlier and lasted longer. So, I concluded that everything had to be moved out immediately. During the long process of hauling materials out no one showed up to help...I wonder why? My wife said she would go up and help me, but I told her she wouldn't want to see a grown man crying as he went up and down a mountain.

The false claim.

I now have a funny looking cabin in my back yard. Never have I looked for another adventure on that piece of property, since the acknowledgment of being a claim jumper shames me.

The Alien

It was August 28, 1982, the opening of archery season. Jerry, myself, and two hunters from Michigan were heading out of Silverton on a bow hunting expedition. The plan was to take the jeep trail through Stony Pass up over the Continental Divide, then down the mountain to Pole Creek where it joins the headwaters of the Rio Grande River. The Ford truck and horse trailer bounced along the dirt road, bottoming out several times before we parked on a hill above Pole Creek. The four of us got out to stretch our legs. After hours of the noise of the laboring truck in our ears the silence was deafening, but that's why we're here.

Colorado has more diversity of terrain than almost any comparable land area on the continent. At this time I was outfitting the Rio Grande Tract, and this was to be a drop camp located at the confluence of Pole and West Pole Creek on the east side of the Divide. Hunters in this region must share an independence that such wide-open spaces bring. The vastness of the wilderness will claim you. We were on the fringe of the Wiminuchi Wilderness, a 500,000 acre expanse of roadless wonderland.

We packed the animals and headed out. The horses were in fine shape, almost too fat. The days were already short, and their coolness even at noon made traveling easy. The trail wove a meandering thread up a gentle grade eventually emerging above the pine and aspen forests. Pristine serenity! There may

Supper's ready.

be more sensible and practical obsessions than hunting and enjoying the high country, but to me, none are more spiritually rewarding.

We followed a distinct trail until we crossed a high ridge and dropped into the drainage of West Pole Creek, which was to be our campsite. After familiarizing the hunters with area and setting up camp, I would check the game trails.

I pointed out some spoor near the site that appeared fresh; I figured it had been made two days earlier, sometime before 8 a.m. The clue was grains of sand stuck to the grass where the elk hooves had flattened it. For the sand to have adhered, the grass must have been wet, and the most recent dew had occurred two days earlier. The elk passed that day before the sun burned off the moisture. The more you observe, the more you enjoy!

One of our bow hunters in a blind.

We explained to the hunters that though their immediate surroundings were strange, they would be able to orient themselves by familiar mountain peaks in the distance. After gathering firewood and fixing up the camp, Jerry and I would leave the hunters to themselves for a week and then pick them up Friday.

There was only an hour of daylight left as we started back to our vehicles, a three-hour ride. As we lost altitude on the trip downstream the spruce and aspen that were just scrub further up the creek became thicker and taller. A half-moon cast shadows on the dark landscape after two hours on the trail. I was dozing in the saddle when the usually trustworthy lead horse spooked, jumping four feet off the trail and taking Jerry's and my mount as well. The other horses went into a panicked dash

downhill. We crashed through the willows in a pitch-black ride for our lives. Boulders, tangles, creeks, deadfalls, it seemed like nothing would stop our charge away from the trail. When I finally got that horse turned the others were dancing and throwing their heads, not wanting to go back to the trail.

I hollered back at Jerry, "What in thunder happened?"

"There's something on the trail," he spoke haltingly, "about eight feet tall… light blue, luminous… It's huge, but I didn't see anything like a head or limbs. I think it's an alien!"

When we finally calmed the horses down we dismounted and cinched up our saddles but didn't do anything. For a few minutes we waited, until the horses got their wind, then maneuvered them over to a big cedar tree. Jerry held the horses, which were snorting, tossing their heads, and still trembling all over. He let me go up the rise to check out this alien being or what ever it was.

Even from the vantage point I could see nothing; the question still remained. What had spooked them? Surely it was nothing natural to the trail that would frighten them like that. I could see nothing what so ever, but I still wasn't quite ready to mount up and ride away. I stood for a couple minutes and listened but couldn't hear anything, so I decided to take my flashlight and walk the trail to investigate.

91

I would walk some and then flash the light up the dark trail. Soon I felt myself getting scared. An alien!

Then up ahead about thirty yards, glowing in the moonlight, was a huge figure, eight feet tall, four feet wide, no marks or recognizable configuration, but with a light blue glow.

Though my mind was racing, the advice I had always given my children kept asserting itself: the fears coming from your imagination are much worse than fears coming from reality. That didn't seem to help. It's good advice for others, but this was me. I was a nervous parent seeing a baby crawl through a cow pasture.

I had no gun with me, so out came my hunting knife. With knife in hand and trembling worse than the horses, I proceeded up the trail. I had read about alien abductions in trashy tabloids, but no spaceship had ever materialized. I hollered at it but no response came from the object. As I approached, it became clear that there were no arms, legs or head.

Suddenly a shrill squeal came from the alien, and I fell to my knees, my nerves gone. I started up the trail on hands and knees, babbling Lord knows what. The alien was now yelling in a human voice and began to transform into a standing man being swallowed up to his neck by a blue blob. Sometimes it takes forever for the obvious to crystallize into a logical perception. I just stood there shaking, until I realized I was seeing a man standing up in a blue silk sleeping bag.

The man, a bow hunter, told me he had walked up the trail,

become tired, and had laid down in his sleeping bag. All tucked in for the night he fell asleep. Awakened by what he thought was a herd of elk coming down the trail (it was actually us), he jumped up fearing he was about to be trampled. He just stood and listened to the brush snapping and animals running. Though he could see nothing, he feared for his life, and as I came back to the trail, he began hollering to scare away whatever was coming up through the brush toward him. When I went back for the horses, I told Jerry it was an alien, "but I scared him away, and he left in his spaceship."

There must be an outdoor experience somewhere in which everything goes smoothly as planned with no disasters, but I think it is yet to be found.

We hauled in the picnic table—a nice touch.

Campfire Stories

Some of the best camping fun comes at night when everybody gathers around the campfire. A major aspect of good outfitting, aside from camp cooking and being away from work a few days, is sitting around the fire telling and listening to stories. The following are a few tales I have shared.

"Pike and Minnows"

Put some pike in a large tank of water. Put some minnows in the tank, but keep the pike and minnows separated by a glass shield inserted between them. The pike will naturally go for the minnows since they dearly love them, their favorite food; but they won't get a one because they bump into the invisible partition. The pike will keep trying—five times, ten times, maybe even fifty times; then they give up. When they give up remove the glass wall, letting the minnows swim freely among the pike. The pike are still hungry. So what happens next?

The pike will not strike the minnows. They will starve to death with all that food around them. Why? They have gotten into their heads *(learned helplessness)* that they cannot get at the minnows. Even though the *conditions* that led to their *original failure* have changed, the pike can't realize that the minnows are now available.

There are people like the pike who have an idea or a dream in their heads. It may have been a good dream, but conditions kept them from making it a reality. It changes to a bad dream of unfulfilled wishes. Conditions may change, but the dream remains stuck in their heads. In a way they starve to death.

Moral—Examine your dreams; the minnows may be all around you.

"Bus Ride"

I was teaching and coaching football in Olathe, Colorado. It was a Friday, and we had a game in Bloomfield, New Mexico. In the Southwest distance seems a minor concern, the idea being to match teams from communities of like size and schools of similar enrollment. This, however, was a long road trip.

I wanted to go elk hunting the next day, so my buddy, Jerry, said that he would take the horses up to Silverton, and I could meet him there on the way back from Bloomfield.

The chartered bus with coaches and team headed out in the afternoon traveling south through Montrose on Highway 550 to Ouray, then to the remote mountain berg of Silverton on the "Million Dollar" Highway, across a high pass, down to Durango and then over the border to New Mexico. During the trip I sat in the back and talked with the athletes about the game, trying to keep them focused on the mission. Two other coaches were sitting up front.

Our professional driver was moving us at a pretty good clip, flying around the curves and pushing the bus on the straightaways. This stretch of highway rises from 5,800 feet to 13,000 feet and back down through curves marked 20 m.p.h. Some of the players were questioning the driver's skills and indicated a bit of concern. I tried to play down the situation, directing their attention back toward our mission, but I did keep one eye on the road.

We got there, played the game, and happened to win. Now for the trip back.

It was 10 o'clock when we left Bloomfield, and after stopping to eat in Durango, we headed back up the mountains for our return trip. Most in the group were tired, the other coaches were up front, and many of the players were catching a few winks. Some of the players in the back with me were rehashing the game, but again the subject of the bus speed and the curving roads became the topic of conversation. Now, almost at midnight, was my chance. Goading them along in their indignation at the dangerous driving, about fifteen minutes from Silverton, I told them that if this driver did not slow down, I was getting off the bus. I pretended to be more and more excited and on the curve just before the little town, I announced to my little group, "I am not going to ride another mile with this driver on this bus," and walked to the front past the sleeping players and coaches.

I quietly explained to the driver that I wanted to get off, as I had folks waiting for me. He stopped the bus without a word, and I walked out into the darkness in the middle of nowhere. As I watched the bus leave, I could see players with their noses pressed to the window, others shouting, "Mr. Chappell got off the bus! Mr. Chappell got off!"

Riding up the trail toward the wilderness, I kept thinking, "Lord, I hope I told at least one of those coaches, I was planning to get off in Silverton tonight."

"Macho Man"

In the early 1980s before *Unit 76,* when the Rio Grande country of Colorado became a Designated Trophy Area, I had the highest outfitting permit issued in Colorado, our camp being at 12,200 feet elevation.

My wife, an orthodox worrier, twice had called the sheriff to search for us when we did not come home on time. Once when we had driven the truck off the side of the mountain and walked eight miles through a storm, we ended up in the only open building in Silverton, the Imperial Hotel and Bar. We were sitting at the bar, begging for any bite of food that could be had, the chef having gone home at 11 PM. The door flew open and the sheriff walked up to our table and said, "Mr. Reynolds, Mr. Chappell?"

We look at each other wondering how he knew us.

"Your wife called, and since I find most 'lost hunters' right here at the bar, I came here first."

With memories of red-faced explanations to our spouses of the caprice of nature, Jerry and I decided to take our wives into the backcountry to show them where we were and what it was like during hunting season. The unknown is scary, and it's much worse staying at home not knowing what's happening than it is actually going through a tough situation. We would give them a firsthand experience of what goes on and what we deal with.

Part of the plan was to let the women ride the horses while climbing uphill; and the men would ride on the level, since we trailered only two horses. Up and over the ridges we climbed. One particular climb was a gut-buster rising to a high plateau with a small pond where a sheepherder friend usually camped while grazing his flock. Upon arriving at the top, the women got off, and we mounted up to ride the into the basin meadow. Riding along my buddy and I talked about bygone hunts. Rounding a bend in the trail we approached the shepherd sitting on a rock in the sun only saying a brief "howdy" as we were in a bit of a hurry. He watched us ride by, and then seeing the women puffing down the trail behind us, he jumped up and yelled with two thumbs in the air, "Macho man, macho man!"

We probably gained a great deal in the eyes of that old Basque. We were real men from that day forward.

"The In-laws"

I received a phone call from my two sons-in-law saying they were coming to the ranch for a visit, and they wished to go back into the mountains for a four-day pack trip with horses—just us guys.

Not being a novice to packing into the backcountry, I realized when there are three people in the group one will be the scapegoat, usually the person who brings the food and cooks the meals. To protect myself from the obvious I gave them one condition: "I'll get the food and everything ready for the trip," I said, "but the first person to say one word of complaint about the food will have to cook for the rest of the trip."

After all agreed, over the phone, to that one rule, preparations began. I told my wife she could bet I would not be cooking for much of this trip. I always like to use my brain—it's the little things that count. My favorite recipe—eat out!

As we started out that first morning before daylight, I cautioned both of them, "Tie those slickers behind the saddle, handy 'cause we'll probably need them, but secure because if you loose 'em you have a problem." I hate having people drop my slickers on the trail because they don't watch what they're doing. I'm usually following along behind with the pack horse and gear, and have to stop, get down, and manage the pack animal that acts up like it's never seen a slicker in the middle of the path.

Well anyway, after nine hours of riding along the Continental Divide Trail we came to the old abandoned mining settlement called Beartown, where we would spend the night. After we took care of the horses, the boys sat down on a log expecting me to fix something to eat. To son-in-law number one, I gave a slice of bread, a tin cup of water and a can of Vienna Sausages (those pale wieners made of pork snouts and scraps from the slaughterhouse floor packed in gelatinous grease). The other received a slice of bread, a cup of water and a can of beef tripe (I made a trip to a specialty store, just for him). For myself, I began with a cold Pepsi from the cold pack in my saddlebag; then I laid out a gourmet turkey dinner—a drumstick, cranberry sauce, dressing and peach cobbler for dessert. After all, we never said we would all eat the same food.

The first young man looked over at the other, back to his food, then over to mine. The first words out of his mouth were, "Man I love these little wieners!" as he sucked the grease off his fingers. The other one just nodded and spread a layer of slimy, greenish beef tripe on his bread and began to eat. The thought of those guys eating that stuff after a long day's ride on an empty stomach almost made me regurgitate my gourmet meal. Smiling, my younger son-in-law looks over at our tack and back at me and says, "Where's your slicker that's supposed to be on the back of your saddle?"

The next three days I spent cooking decent food when I wasn't riding in the rain with my head sticking out of a garbage bag.

"The Young Hunter, or 'Finders, Keepers'"

During the early '80s Jerry and I were outfitting a drop camp for elk in the Pole Creek area of the Rio Grande. On the way out, after setting up camp, we spoke to a father and son who were hunting in the area.

The fourteen year-old boy had shot a five-point elk the first day and had tracked it for eight hours unsuccessfully. Three days later another hunter from a party camped next to them found the carcass and cut off the horns, the body heat having spoiled the meat. He carried the horns back to camp, and the boy claimed them. The hunter refused to give the boy his rack, saying, "I found it; it's mine."

Listening to his account, it was evident the rack meant much to the boy, so my buddy and I went over to reason with the hunting party and the guy who found the rack. We got the same story; the rack was his.

I looked at Jerry, and he just nodded his head. I decided a long time ago, every man must know what principles he is willing to die for. That's just the way it is, but you must choose your battles carefully.

Walking over to the horns I picked them up and strolled away, not saying a word. My buddy stood on the path facing the group and quietly said, "You better know when you are well off."

We went to the father and son's camp, gave the boy back his rack and suggested we camp there until they were ready to leave.

Seven years later we met the same boy, hunting the same area, but now he was a big strapping twenty-one-year-old man with a resolve that no one would ever take his elk from him now.

"Sunday Dinner"

Back in the 1960s my buddy Jerry and I were teachers in Michigan. Neither of us had much money, since we were both raising families and like most folks during that time, we had a place for every penny. Both of us needed a break after school was out, so we planned a fishing trip to Canada. We came up with a hundred and forty dollars that would buy our licenses, bait, gas, two quarts of oil, and the food we could scrounge from our wives kitchen pantries.

Off we went to a fishing spot above Lake Superior in the Canadian woods. We fished for five days with fair luck, but with our food running low we had to return. We figured the money for trip would be just enough for gas; we had the can of oil, but no cash left for food. We had held out until we were down to the last can of pork and beans for a fourteen-hour trip, but we had not eaten in the last ten hours.

It was a beautiful Sunday morning, and we traveled along the east side of Lake Superior heading home *hungry*. As we drove along I kept pulling into parks and picnic areas on the roadside. Jerry kept saying, " Why are we pulling into all these parks? They are beautiful, but let's get home!"

I motored on down the road and pulled into yet another park. Viewing a large group gathered for a picnic outing, we placed ourselves at the next table, in a spot closest to the grandma of the family. Trying to look dignified, we got out our can of beans and a single spoon. We passed the spoon back and forth consuming our shared Sunday dinner, one pitiful can of pork and beans.

It wasn't long before grandma came over and asked what the situation was. We politely explained. It wasn't long before we were enjoying mashed potatoes, fried chicken and all the fixin's. And when we departed we had a box lunch that could have lasted for days. Thank the Lord for kind-hearted grandmas and a little insight into human nature.

"The Great Equalizer"

On a fishing trip in the mountains with a group of rugged outdoorsmen, fishing during the day and enjoying each other's company around meals, we were having a great time. During the evening hours we sat around the campfire spinning yarns of wilderness adventures. We all came to the conclusion that there was nothing in nature we feared other than the whims of mountain weather.

There were six of us men sitting around the embers with enough firepower to reverse the outcome of the Battle of the Alamo. No bear, mountain lion, or other wild creature could intimidate or challenge our presence. Along about 10 o'clock we retired to a sheepherder's tent and crawled in our sleeping bags lined against the back wall. The question came up, "What if a bear walked into camp and stuck his head in the tent, what would we do?"

One of the guys said, "My 30-06 would be out and firing, and my .357 would be next." That didn't make the rest of us feel to good, but I got to sleep with one eye cocked. Around midnight it started to rain and then another noise came from the grocery stash. Someone flicked on a flashlight, and we watched a skunk open a sack of our potato chips and help himself to our food. Lying in the back of our three-sided tent we watched as each time we played the light on him he would do his tail-up handstand and wait. Turning the light away he would go back to eating. When we turned the light back on him he raised his tail and waited for our next move. Lights off!

One of the guys pulled out his revolver and said, "I'm going to shoot him."

"Lord, no!" None of us wanted to be sleeping outside in the rain if that skunk got off a shot before or after the hero. There we sat, trapped with a formidable foe having his way with our groceries. Another fellow says, "I'll throw my shoe off to the side; maybe it will spook him." But that idea also was voted down.

There we sat in the dark for two hours with no good options, while this little creature enjoyed our food. Believe me; nature has a way of humbling a person. There can always be a skunk in the works.

"Chicken Hawk"

Which reminds me of a story one of my students told about a neighbor of his. It seems this neighbor had been missing an occasional chicken. One morning while out in the barn he heard a racket in the hen yard. Hurrying outside he saw a large hawk carrying one of his layers up and out of the pen. Furiously he ran to the house and grabbed his shotgun, loading as he ran back out the door. Once outside all he could do was watch the hawk flapping away, out of range by this time.

Determined to catch the culprit the next time, he placed the gun by the barn door and carried the shells in his pocket every morning when he went about his chores. Three days later he again heard the racket in the chicken yard. Running out of the barn, loading on the way, he saw the hawk struggling to gain altitude with a heavy rooster. It couldn't quite make it over the top and hung up on a fold of the chicken wire fence. The farmer set his gun down and shucked off his jacket with which he enveloped the hawk. His anger giving way to revenge, his great mind developed a plan to give the miscreant his just reward.

He stuffed the bundled bird into a half-full feed sack with just his talons hanging out and a turn of twine to hold him there. Then he went to his stash of dynamite and pulled out not one, but two sticks, a fuse, and cap. Back at the bird he tied the charge to its feet and lit the fuse, taking it out of the sack, he flung it in the air and watched with great satisfaction as it climbed and circled. Then, as if thinking to get rid of the hissing mess on its feet, it swooped down to land on the ridge of the barn roof.

I understand some folk's mode of thinking when they live with predators on a daily basis, but perhaps that farmer will reconsider his values and join human society, if not the Humane Society.

"Branding Elk"

Another friend of mine told me about a rancher who loved to fool around with wildlife during his daily routines on the ranch. One such opportunity would occur each spring as father, son, and grandpa would check the fences in the high country, before bringing up the cattle for spring grazing.

The ritual was for the father and son to look for elk calves along the draws and creeks, ignoring grandpa's lectures about staying on the job, doing their work, and leaving the wildlife alone. Undeterred in their quest for excitement the two regularly stopped, bailed out of the truck, ran toward a small sleeping elk calf, and pounced on it. They'd check its plumbing, and if it happened to be a bull calf one would start a fire, heat a bit of barbed wire, and put their brand on it.

Over the years they had great fun telling people who hunted that area above their ranch and shot a bull with their brand, that it was part of their private herd and just compensation should be forthcoming. This was all fun and games until the Fish and Game Department came around checking out some of the stories. They explained that persons harassing wildlife could be arrested and fined, especially for putting claim to publicly owned wildlife.

"Surely someone was putting this ranch's brand on elk just to get them in trouble. Most rational people would know better than to put their own brand on wild game," the rancher contended. And the game warden left with only the implied warning.

Of course, next spring the same ritual took place, but now it was even more fun. Bouncing along the mountain roads the boy on lookout spotted an elk. "There, in the tall grass right along the creek," the father hollers. Out of the truck they bound.

But the grandpa yells, "You come back here, or I'm leaving you guys to walk home."

The boy pounced on the half-hidden bull calf, and the game proceeded with a small fire and all the preparations nearly complete, when down the hill comes a mother cow elk. With fire in her eye and murder in her heart, she charges at the distress call of her offspring. The boy found a climbable aspen and was up in a flash. The father stood behind two smaller trees with the intent of keeping them between him and the mad mama. She tore around the boy's tree with the father standing awe struck by her speed and agility. She doubled back to his trees, and he knew he had no chance of getting around them faster than she, so up between them he shinnies, holding them together, hoping the two saplings will support his weight high enough above the elk which is standing on her hind legs, doing her damnedest to sink an elk's tooth in his cohones.

The boy, alert to the gravity of the situation, calls the dogs from the back of the truck. These were a mixed breed of cow dogs, trained and able to intimidate and control a 2000-pound bull. Up the draw lope three ferocious hounds intent on persuading the mother to leave, but within seconds the dogs are butted, chopped, and kicked into whining, snarling submission under the truck. The two fellows hanging in the trees watched as the cow came back and stood under their shaky sanctuary while grandpa loaded up the dogs and drove off waving, "See ya about dark when the work's done."

Hunting: Notes from my Journal

When I talk of hunting or fishing I'm talking about a special class of experience. There's nothing wrong with coming home with little to show for your efforts, though success is measured in many different ways.

Every year the average hunter, the one without big money, is pushed to find land to hunt on; and every year the old-style hunters who carry on the traditions of the past become fewer. The new hunter is brought a little closer to the radio, television, microwave, and other creature comforts of lodges all in the proximity of imitation hunters. As he comes closer to the agents of standardized society he depends more and more on them for his amusement and less and less on his skills, senses, ability and memory. I detect decay in the art of enjoying the outdoors.

Hundreds of thousands of words have been written about outdoor adventures, mostly glossed over and hyped for commercial or aesthetic reasons. An outdoor experience can and probably should be a serene, undisturbed perception and reflection to take home and enjoy forever—a chance to slow down or turn back the clock.

A truly enjoyable, time altering experience requires an adventurous spirit, a thirst for knowledge, and a romantic sense of awe for the land you are discovering. One must take in the vast panoramas, the closely viewed wonders, the powers of weather, and revel in the freedom to discover. The remem-

Just contemplating great thoughts.

brance of an outing should encompass the fullness of life spent in field or stream—the hopes of the morning, the observations of the day, and the evaluations at day's end. Yes, including the moments when things went left of center and fell short of expectations. Within the sportsman's journal lies the direction of the future and perspectives more precious than money. More

Morning.

than a tallying of fish or game taken, it is a reflection of how a life is lived.

A first step leading to good memories is developing a reverence for the past, or at least a conscious understanding of the hardships miners, trappers and mountain men endured.. They struggled daily, encountering great hardships just to stay alive, while all the modern outdoorsman has to do is find his way back to camp, stumble through a clutter of camping parapher-

Evening.

nalia, stoke the fire (or light the Coleman), eat his packaged food and crawl into the sleeping bag under his space blanket or pop up tent. One might not have been raised to develop a heightened awareness of the world around us like our hunter-gatherer forbearers, but one can revive these skills if willing to give up the numbing chase of material wealth in soul killing cities. Cease the hyperactive, attention deficit, fondness for gadgets and thrill-a-minute virtual unreality games. We can even pass some old time values on if we can wean our children from mindless pastimes. Let's leave the walls of the workplace and the noise of the city and find the treasure of enjoyment outdoors.

If you keep your journals with total and complete honesty, always with an eye out for the unexpected and unforeseen, you will see how God lives and works in the uncertain freedom of this world, as we do. The only guarantees in this life are in the next.

"Some Thoughts on Conservation"

Hunting is a necessary part of conservation. We will conserve what we love. We love what we know, and we know what we have experienced. Spread the word about how crucial hunting and sport fishing are to the future of wildlife and indeed to our future on the planet!

In Colorado, The Division of Wildlife is an agency of state government that doesn't get a dime of tax money. About three-fourths of its annual income derives from the sale of hunting licenses. If not for hunters there would be very little game in Colorado today. Thanks to them and the wildlife managers they support, animal populations are in better shape than ever before. The state needs to harvest animals to keep the size of the herds within the carrying capacity of their habitat. U.S. Forest Service records from 1910 indicated that only 500 to 1000 elk remained in Colorado, concentrated in ten small herds, the

Ready for rain.

largest being in the headwaters of the White and Gunnison Rivers. Ninety years later Colorado boasts of approximately 200,000 elk.

Not all new management programs have been effective. Contraception measures have failed to control deer populations. States without a balance of predators, hunters, and prey have had to formulate plans to bait and shoot excess animals to control herd numbers. Big game can be thought of as undomesticated cattle that must be managed. The death of some individuals is necessary for the life of the herd. Hunting, as it is controlled today, is not a destructive force but an ecologically sound annual harvest. It would be ecologic suicide to eliminate sport hunting.

Urban sprawl continues to take a toll on wild lands, so maximizing our management of the remaining acreage will be a necessity if we are to have balanced game populations. No one, but the hunters and the governmental agencies they support, can or are likely to do it.

"Hunting Families"

We are going to learn that what I call "homesickness" is an important issue in the enjoyment of the outdoors, especially if we have loved ones at home. It has little to do with what is going on outside a person, but much to do with what's going on inside us, one of the last unexplored regions for most folks.

We must teach our young people to stop, look, and listen—to enjoy beauty by shutting off the computer and the television for a weekend. Show someone you love a new world of magic that has been there for years waiting for you to enter and enjoy. If a kid who lives in the town or suburbs can jump on his bicycle and go a mile or so to fish, we will all benefit. Share your feelings with your children and spouse so they will understand your vision more clearly.

Men need not worry that their women folk are not up to the challenges of the outdoors. After studying survival rates of people lost in the wild, a University of Washington researcher concludes that most women are better equipped physically to endure nature's hardships. The general basics of smaller body size and slower metabolic rate means less food is required. More body fat helps insulate against the cold and conserves energy.

Longtime Michigan friends and hunters.

Perhaps the female's reluctance to take risks and to act aggressively may also aid in survival by minimizing accidental injuries and death. Remembering the infamous (for cannibalism) Donner Party, 35 of 82 died: 57 percent of the men, versus 28 percent of the women. So much for that "weaker sex" label (discounting the probability of chivalrous, self sacrificing men).

"Learning"

Reading, as well as a recollection of past reading, can add much to your store of experience. Browsing bookstores is a form of hunting in itself, and the revival of this practice can open possibilities for enjoyment that buying books on the Internet cannot match. I encourage hunters, young and older, to read. Even adults can benefit from a course on ecology at their local community college; or they can read a book on the ecology of the state in which you are hunting and study the weather and the climatology of the region. The Division of Wildlife publishes informative tracts on all aspects of local wildlife. Through reading one can gain insights from other's experiences that otherwise would be lost.

The stories one can learn from are not always found in books, so I encourage folks to learn from each other. There's a story that comes with every hunt. Sharing in it mentally or physically with friends can be a wonderful experience. Hunt with others but associate yourself with quality people who will make the right moves when things go wrong. Things can and do go wrong! Go with folks whose experience can make you look good. Know when to defer to their judgment and get out of the way. Trust your own common sense in most cases; ignoring it results in wasted time, unnecessary hardship, and, in some cases, disaster. Listen to the most experienced outdoorsman among you.

I have noticed that some people who have just gotten back from hunting avoid other folks who also just get back from a hunt because they don't want to hear others talk about their experiences, or worse, be invited to see their slides or videos. It's

Spotting elk across the canyon.

the down side of bragging, "the first liar doesn't stand a chance." Some stories are not worth listening to and still they persist: "The Fish and Game Department plane deliberately scatters all the animals just before the season opens." "The 'trophy elk' turns out to be a mule or cow, when brought to the game check station." When I talked to the Division of Wildlife *terrestrial resources manager* who had information from a heck of a lot of check stations, he said both are "just a couple of stories."

In my writings you will not (I hope) find just trivial bits of information. My intent is to stir your imagination, not insult your intelligence. Read between the lines too. If you get strange intimations that you have been there before in another life, you are processing the information you're gathering. What ever it is you do, you can become better at it if you just keep thinking and learning.

"Where and When to Hunt"

Realize and accept that there are a great many hunters today. Many a would-be hunter feels he cannot get far enough away to be safe or find truly wild game or experience the solitude they seek. The answer is not to give up on hunting because everyone is going but to go some place beyond the convenient camping spots. If you want to find game, you can—if you are willing to spend the time and endure some pain with the sport. Hunting's history is full of hardship stories. Perhaps you are most interested in the tales of the lone sportsman who stalked his quarry aided only by his wits and skill as a woodsman. Unless you are really experienced, I recommend you go with someone who is. You can find good locations if you have time to travel and scout the high country; then come back and hunt it. If you don't have that kind of time, find a small-scale outfitter, one who doesn't take large numbers of hunters. Learn from his experience and scouting, and enjoy the hunt with him.

Have you heard this? "I've been through every inch of this country and I ain't seen any animals." This most often comes from an out of shape guy perched on an expensive and noisy ATV. He has been sputtering around your area since first light,

Riding back from a day's hunt.

and the fact of the matter is *he's the reason* neither of you have seen any game. Try to find an area that is tough to get in and out, but one you can hunt, rather than one that is easy to get to but tough to hunt.

One of the best places to hunt is on timber sale areas that are two to six years old. The succulent new growth vegetation attracts most grazing and browsing animals like elk and mule deer. The United States Forest Service can and will give you that information.

Riding out with a packsaddle to bring a downed elk back to camp.

If you can have only one time to go hunting, pick the rut. The weather is acceptable, elk are bugling, and you will hear them even if you don't see them. But you probably will; males are foolish compared to other times of the year. Regardless of how you hunt—bow, black powder, or rifle—that's the time to hunt. There are perhaps more sensible and practical obsessions than hunting and fishing, like earning a million dollars, but nothing is more satisfying and rewarding than your memories of time spent in the outdoors.

The Quarry Always Holds the Cards

The tale of most hunting trips should be entitled "Doofus Goes Hunting." Many times I have thought myself a fool, an idiot, an addlepated nincompoop, and a simpleton. Usually this was in the early days of my hunting life, as I sat freezing in a deer blind, slogging back to camp in a downpour, or shivering in a clammy sleeping bag. It was then I would think of the creature comforts of a warm bed, television, or a hot meal by the fireplace at home. Now I sit among those creature comforts and think of the comfort that nature can bring.

Men spend so much of their time trying to get ahead, proving themselves in competition with others. In hunting we also compete with ourselves: always bettering our preparation for the challenges we will face from the game, the terrain, or the weather. Through the sport we experience an emotion hard to describe to anyone who hasn't experienced such an appreciation of life, that sense of discovery that comes while following trails into the wilderness. In hunting, my friends and I have traveled to nearly inaccessible areas of backcountry only to come home without game. Other times we have returned to the same area and found phenomenal hunting. But always the living world is a single, beautiful working entity.

Life is for the living, but the past is another reality where a person can spend time with buddies who live only in the minds of those who remember. With our friends all that is expected is

A long ride up the Continental Divide.

that one listen: no advice, no words of wisdom, similar experiences, money, assistance, proffered expertise, or even sympathy ... just a minute or two to listen to a friend's experience. In our advanced technological society with its sophisticated communication, we still suffer a shortage of listeners. Automated telephone messages offer options we can't use, and answer questions we haven't asked. We ourselves practice tuning out unwanted interruptions more than active listening.

Most people enjoy the camaraderie that goes on before, during, and after a hunt, but it is best when you go with someone you trust and admire who can share the joys ;of the outdoors. Hunting should be a pleasant social occasion, so one does not hunt with just anyone who thinks they want to go out and kill a bigger trophy. One goes out to hunt to escape to a green, beautiful place, think clearly, revive the spirit, and recharge the creative batteries. One does not need the competition of the workplace brought to the outdoors. The benefits of the outdoor experience often depend on the qualities of the people you hunt with.

One hunt in particular comes to mind. We were outfitting the Rio Grande headwaters in Colorado. The group was made up of Texans, friends of Don McMurry from Nacogdoches. He had hunted with me before and all of us wanted Don to get a nice bull.

The first day was spent exploring the higher elevations, hoping to find the master herd bull. We had to be careful at those heights; up here summer and winter can come in the same day. Hunting all that day with just enough daylight to get back to camp we saw only one small bull. The next day we climbed another shoulder of the mountain, again to no avail. Along

Sometimes high.

about noon ominous clouds warned us to return to camp.

We shared our lunch in the company of two Basque shepherds whose caravans put out thick smoke that rolled up the mountain at our back in the brisk autumn breeze. Nine horses, ours and theirs, shared the grass at the edge of a clearing overlooking a mile wide meadow. We ate watching a south-facing mountain covered only by tundra, lush grass with no cover; but what a beautiful sight as the cloud shadows chased across the waves of green. Sitting there, enjoying the scenery, sopping up the last of a Brunswick stew with homemade bread, we noticed two elk coming around the mountain, but neither had horns.

We watched casually, as the elk watched intently, looking ahead and then back over the trail. They wandered down the mountainside and through the creek and started up our side. We all held our breath as they continued walking to within fifty feet of the camp! Suddenly they looked directly at us, as if noticing the camp at the edge of the timber for the first time. They bolted, circling away and entering the woods behind us.

Don turned to me and exclaimed, "If one of those had been a bull, I could have shot him from the table while I was eating." We all had a big laugh at his wishful exuberance.

Finishing our lunch with a cup of coffee, we noticed another elk coming around the mountain appearing to be following the other two. I put the field glass on the elk and saw horns as he came from behind a boulder. "Now is your chance," I told Don, "to shoot an elk on your lunch hour."

Positioning his rifle on a rolled up jacket on the table, he waited. As the elk came off the mountain we watched him grow larger, seeing his massive neck sawing the rack from side to side as he tested the air. From the distance at which we first saw him it took twenty minutes for the elk to cross the creek and start up the hill toward our camp. He kept his nose to the ground following a path. He walked to within fifty yards of camp before looking up at our horses that had begun stomping and fidgeting at his approach. I watched out of the corner of my eye from behind the tree where I was trying to stay out of sight. He turned, and Don hunkered down at the table and shot. This bull

Sometimes low.

proved to be one of the largest elk we have ever taken from this area.

There are times when the hunters have all filled their permits by 3 p.m. the first day. Other times in this same area we have been skunked and blown away by the unpredictable Colorado weather. All I can say is: Go early, stay late, and move as quietly as you can since animals have a way of showing up when and where you least expect them. Being in the right place at the right time is the trick. But you have to be out in the woods to be in the right place.

Shooting

I have been involved in numerous discussions on guns and shooting techniques over the years, school age through thirty years of outfitting, and here is the distillation of many bull sessions and questions answered about what and how to shoot. Much of this, when reduced to simple terms, may seem contradictory; so think of it as paradox or Zen.

To be able to shoot straight—just shoot enough to get the feel of the gun going off. Don't aim at any target that is too minute. Better a pie tin than a beer can; it's nice to have the reinforcement of hitting what you are aiming at. But the first task is to learn that the gun isn't going to hurt you. Flinching is due to problems in the head, so I am not going to say much more to add to that headfull, except *squeeeeze* the trigger!

Like any true gun person, I can't name one really favorite gun or caliber. All have their purposes, though some have no business in the woods with sportsmen. Most discussions about guns and ammunition are because of people's need for points of reference: a base to start from, points to draw from regardless of their effect on the hunt. Don't over gun yourself. You must first hit where you aim. Whatever gun you can do that with, use it. Most hunters don't shoot enough to know how really well their firearms can perform. My son-in-law, Todd Richardson, who outfits with me, and I have settled on the .270 with loads of 130 to 150 grain. Many people say that's too small for elk, but I do not recall ever loosing a wounded animal in over thirty years of hunting elk with a .270.

Sighting is another topic. I find that sighting in dead at 100 yards is best for most big game hunting. For most of the hunters the tendency is to miss high at short distances. It is much easier to compensate high at long distances than low with short shots. With modern high-powered loads the trajectory is flat enough that little or no compensation is necessary at ranges out to about 250 yards. Practice with targets at different yardages. Shoot, shoot, shoot, but know that about 80% of the elk taken by our hunters have been between 100 and 150 yards. I've heard about the 1,000-yard shots too; good campfire stories, and they do happen. My philosophy is hunt better; get close.

Here is a bit of Zen: *shoot quick, shoot slow*. Forget the idea, "If I miss the first shot, I'll get him with the next three." One of the reasons hunters choke is that things happen fast, and game are few. Learn to relax and practice, practice, practice. Don't argue cartridges and guns for game. Gun nuts give themselves hyperactive anxiety attacks. Use whatever gun and ammunition you can hit with; but then, I have watched some of the greatest pie plate killers in the West miss game. Keep it simple.

Hunting Deer and Elk

I hope there will always be hunters and parents with young people in the woods, and sleepless nights before opening day, and dreams of adventure in the wilderness. Then I pick up one of the current hunting magazines and open it to a picture of some guy you wouldn't want to meet, heading for some place you want to keep private until you could afford to go there yourself. And he would be going there with ten other guys you didn't want to share the woods with either. If you want to go hunting, forget all the excuses for not going. Get your buddy and go do it. There is still enough wild country and animals out there, if you can get out to where they are.

Finding good game requires hard work and knowledge of both the country and the animal. Things change when hunting pressure hits the high country. Scouting an area tells you where the animals were before the season opened, but an army of blaze-orange creatures wandering around the habitat changes the ecosystem. "Where are they now?" You ask. "This is all old sign!" The key to finding game is to know where they went or what the animal's response to hunting pressure will be. If you don't have time to gather the information yourself, get an out-fitter and gain the benefit of years of experience and knowledge.

When I am asked, "How do I physically prepare for a hunt?" I usually say forget it; the altitude will make your body adjust to the conditions no matter what kind of shape you are in. If you know you have altitude problems because of your heart or respiration, spend a few days at three to four thousand feet then on to 6,000. When you get tired and the game is hard to find, just keep a positive attitude. Now you are hunting!

Of more concern is hypothermia. Exposure to cold, wet and windy weather can lead to trouble. Watch out for uncontrolled shivering, one of the first signs that a person's core body temperature has been lowered. If cooling is allowed to progress, hypothermia causes lack of coordination, loss of judgment, unconsciousness, and even death. When a person shows that first sign of uncontrolled shivering, they need to get to a warm place, take warm non-alcoholic drinks, and eat quick energy foods.

For most of the questions asked about hunting there are simple answers, and most of them are wrong. The answers are complex. Few deer hunters have gone afield without asking himself, "am I going right past the deer without seeing them?" Let me assure you; you are. Thirty years ago studies were made using radio collared deer that showed a dumb deer might not be so dumb after all. An animal might remain in a wooded draw in the middle of a pasture for up to two days. At night he might come down to pasture, but the morning would always find him back in the higher woods where he knew he had safer cover. Deer would stand behind a butte as hunters approached and then progress around to the opposite side as they passed by, unnoticed by hunters forty yards away. Keep in mind that deer, and this applies to elk too, have a thousand times better sense of smell than ours. Their large swiveling ears collect and funnel sounds into their heads for constant analyses of irregularity and possible danger. They did not survive as a prey species without keen senses.

Even though you are hunting bucks, locate family groups of antlerless deer. Focus on their activity, not the obvious buck signs like rubs and scrapes. That's where they were! Work on your still hunting technique, but if you must stalk deer, here's a tip. Move only when the deer have their head down, feeding. Just before they look up, deer twitch their tails, your signal to stand still or sink down and wait for feeding to start again.

The studies show deer seem to prefer grassland for browsing and resting during the night, and open stands of timber for feeding and resting during daylight hours. Deer use dense stands of timber, especially pine, for resting and hiding but do relatively little feeding; don't ask me why, when they seem to prefer the ornamental pines in my yard above all else. This probably shows why preseason scouting is not as effective as postseason scouting. Hunting pressure and seasonal food sources modify game behavior.

Elk hunting is broken into seasons, and the influences of hunting pressure and weather are key factors in locating game at different times. During bow hunting and muzzleloader seasons, in late August and September, elk are typically banded together on their summer range. That's where you may still find them during the first of rifle season around October 10th, but that changes in a hurry.

During the second season they break away from large groups and start moving away from hunting pressure. They either move uphill to nasty, steep black timber, drop off onto benches where hunters don't walk, or they move down onto private land. Toward the end of second season there is usually a "dead zone" between 8,000 and 9,500 feet elevation. So, if you hunt late season, choose an area next to a high wilderness tract, since the animals will come down, driven by winter snows.

Out-of-staters usually hunt the first season and early in the second. Locals hunt the late season. This is mainly due to weather. The weather is better early, and there are some retarded bulls taken, but the late season offers a chance at the bigger, better animals, as the snows force as yet unhunted herds out of the vast, high wilderness areas.

Late season hunters must be persistent. Keep in mind how elk can survive in hellholes for weeks. Having a very adaptive digestive system they can eat woody vegetation, such as stems and twigs, surviving very well. They will endure much to avoid humans. They don't like you; they think you smell bad! But as you trek for miles, covering enough ground where they're not, you are getting closer to where they are. Persistence also pays when you hit an animal. Track, track, track. A carcass on the ground, out of direct sunlight for twelve hours, at temperatures less than forty degrees, will still be good.

Looking for the big one.

After your hunting trip realize that no one wants to see your slides. You will remember every detail for years to come, but you better remember the important stuff like your anniversary and your wife's birthday, or you may never go hunting again.

General Useful Information
to help you survive and enjoy hunting in the mountains

Colds: Replicated experiments in England indicate that people left shivering outdoors are no more likely to catch a cold than those who stay warm indoors. That's because viruses cause colds, and unless there is a virus out in the cold with you, you won't catch a cold.

Wet feet: Carry garbage bags in your pack. Use them to wade across creeks and other wet areas. They are lighter than boots and you can throw them away (not on the trail please) when they are punctured. Garbage bags have many other possibilities in emergencies.

Getting on a horse: The green horn, even if he knows enough to mount from the "near" or left side, will for a long time persist in climbing into the saddle, hauling himself up by hanging on to the cantle with his right hand. He must release his hold as he swings his right leg over (or wind up with his hand in his crotch). After he has tried that a few times on one of those beasts he calls a "bronco" and knows is an "outlaw," he may realize why a cowgirl never puts a hand on the cantle but grasps the pommel or "horn" she calls it. Perhaps she puts her foot in the stirrup turning it square out or a little twisted to the front, so that when she springs into the saddle it helps her into position even if the horse rears or moves out.

Sleeping out: The tenderfoot, when far enough along in his outdoor education to venture sleeping without a tent, lies down with his head higher than his feet, looking out for what ever may be coming, but with little regard to the wind. The old-timer sleeps with his feet to the wind, so that the bedding will not be blown loose letting in cold blasts around his neck and back.

Don't talk on the trail: Most of the graves along the trail, according to ancient lore, are the final resting places of guides who were talked to death by tourists. Save conversations for the campfire.

First days: Remember during the first days of most adventures when you think you are cracking up with anxieties and worries about what you might have forgotten or ought to have done. Then suddenly your mind will turn the corner, and you can settle down to enjoy it. Hang in there.

Tents: Nature has a way of promoting the motel industry. It always rains on tents. Rainstorms will travel thousands of miles against the prevailing winds for the opportunity to rain on a tent. Tents contain mildew spores, tiny one-celled creatures activated by moisture that immediately start committing acts of aggression. If they don't give you an allergy attack they will at least make you think you are sleeping in a giant unwashed gym sock. Sure is nice to have a safe source of heat in your tent.

Rest whenever you can!

Baby wipes: They are great for cleaning hands after field dressing game; they work better than anything I found for messy hands, and they cover odor. Great too for saddle weary butts.

Ice for the chest: Ice for hunting fishing or camping will last so much longer if you make it in gallon milk jugs with the addition of half cup of salt to the gallon. Freeze the jugs for several days as salt-water freezes at about zero F ^{o}. It takes longer but lasts longer.

Colorado in the Good Times

I have hunted and fished from Alaska to Texas, New England to California, but in my estimation no state has greater outdoor opportunity than Colorado. And when the "good old days" are remembered years from now, they will be the first decades of the twenty-first century. Colorado's elk population is the largest it has been in sixty years, and deer are coming back under good management. My stories of hunting and fishing were drawn from the experiences of a mature and professional sportsman who had a lifetime of pleasure from the woods, water, and open spaces of many parts of the country. Many of the results of trips have been average; some expeditions produced no game, and some were with full limits. The latter are not necessarily the ones to be remembered forever. All animal populations will fluctuate with the cycles of nature, but the opportunities for hunters are here and now. Decades from now Colorado big game hunters will tell their grandchildren about hunting during this period of year after year record harvests.

Ask most Americans to name five presidents, and chances are Theodore Roosevelt will be among them. He had a phenomenal passion for the outdoors and wild things. I'm not sure if it was T.R. or Thorstein Veblen who said in effect, "We may divide the whole struggle of the human race into two chapters, first the fight to get leisure, and the second, what shall we do with our leisure when we get it." I'd like to believe it was

Roosevelt, who certainly knew how to enjoy his time outdoors and did so much to conserve and preserve nature for future generations to enjoy.

The twentieth century has produced a world of conflicting visions, intense emotions, and unpredictable events. The chances to seize the goodness of life have dwindled as the pace of activity has accelerated. It is hard to grasp the brass ring if the merry-go-round whirls at the speed of light. Electronic media and virtual reality shuffle us through a myriad of experiences that would baffle our ancestors. It produces in us isolation from each other and the reality of human history.

We must establish priorities in experiencing the many sensations that flood us. At the beginning of the century most Americans worked long hours, the twelve-hour day being common. Many folks, especially those caring for livestock, worked seven days a week. At the same time cities were growing and the number of nonagricultural jobs were increasing. As business grew so did our paperwork, but still we said, "We have no lords, for whom we toil, starve and bleed; we are the most perfect society now existing in the world." A popular tune among college students when I was going to school was:

> I sing in praise of college,
> of M.A.s and Ph.D.s
> But in pursuit of knowledge
> We are starving by degrees.

How are we to feed our souls with real food when we are surrounded with processed, packaged synthetics and surrogates?

At night America's big cities are alive with a plethora of sights and sounds. Night in the Colorado mountains is a different story. There, the only sound might be a coyote's howl, and the best entertainment, a safe night's sleep. Out here a "chip" is a small piece of wood, "grass" is what the cows eat, "coke" is a cold drink, and "pot" is what you cook in. Time-sharing still means spending time with friends and family. For some the pursuit of happiness, from the time of Thoreau at least, has been a quest to get back to the basics. While others travel to see the Seven Wonders of the World, I say phooey! The very technology and ease in travel that have made viewing the world's unusual sights commonplace, can also make enjoying your leisure impossible. Sometime after walking a quarter of a mile through a parking lot on a blistering hot day, to stand in line for an hour and a half to get into an event where your participation is limited to observation and ineffective comment (no matter how energetically expressed) you can yet appreciate the outdoors. Stop where you are; nature isn't going anywhere. You are already standing right inside a weird world. There's a creature here, all around you, strange and even terrifying. It is you.

Time has a way of slipping away from us and going on as it pleases. Take control of your time and your life. Live while you are alive and then get ready to die with no regrets.

Backcountry trout.

For me the time of my life has been outdoors in Colorado. Factors linked to enjoying the outdoors are evident in Colorado. This state has the lowest percentage of overweight people. A survey in 1992 of behavioral risks showed "exercise is a key factor ... though not everyone in Colorado is an athlete, most Colorad'ns share moderate levels of exercise." Colorado ranks sixth in states having the fewest sedentary people. We love the outdoors—hunting, hiking, skiing, golfing, and serving folks who come to this great state for sport and recreation.

Clean air is certainly a factor in health and quality of life. Molas Pass in southwest Colorado recently earned the distinction of having the cleanest air in the nation. Using a special monitoring camera, the U.S. Forest Service determined that the

Good And Good For You

—Health information on select wild and domestic meats and fish.

Meat type	Calories	Total Fat	Cholesterol	Saturated Fat
Elk	146	1.9 g	73 mg	.7 g
Deer	153	1.4 g	89 mg	1.1 g
Moose	134	.97 g	78 mg	.3 g
Bison	143	2.4 g	82 mg	.59 g
Lean Roast Beef	239	14.3 g	87 mg	7.2 g
Lean Ham	153	5.8 g	58 mg	7.7 g
Chicken w/o skin	163	3.5 g	85 mg	1.3 g
Salmon	163	5.8 g	87 mg	1.9 g

(all data based on a 3.5-ounce serving)

air here contains the lowest particulate pollution, allowing views that can extend as many as 170 miles.

The diversity of the San Juan Mountains provides various ecosystems, which make suitable habitats for many wildlife species. And there is no better time to be in the mountains than in the fall mating seasons. Of all the large mammals of the West, the majestic elk has the most dramatic and energetic rut, which peaks in late September. A bull elk bugling is one of the most exhilarating sounds in nature. The four or five year-old bull having had good winter and summer food will not only have a thrilling voice, he will have the prized set of antlers you are after.

Who are the folks hunting in Colorado? The majority of elk hunters are employed among the blue-collar ranks. Nearly sixty percent of all elk hunters and fifty-three percent of all hunter types are in this occupational group according to the U.S. Fish and Wildlife Service report (1972). Another interesting statistic—if a person has not hunted by age twenty, he probably will never hunt. The trend in licenses issued suggests that the number of elk hunters will increase in the United States. Nonresident hunters tend to be more successful than resident hunters, though this statistic may be misleading. Motivation and thus actual time spent intensively hunting in the field may be greater for nonresidents than residents.

Let's follow the elk and hunter through a day before the elk have moved to lower country as they do after the snows have accumulated to sixteen inches. The day begins with an active feeding period shortly before first light and continues until the paunch or rumen has been filled. After active feeding the lead cow moves the band to a bedding area with good visibility. The elk settle and begin the process of ruminating or chewing their cuds of the forage consumed earlier. The process may take several hours, after which they remain most of the midday idling about this bedding area. Late afternoon feeding resumes two to three hours before sunset.

The knowledgeable hunter watches the trails on which elk take advantage of the terrain, traveling parallel to exposed ridges and immediately below ridgelines, just under the horizon. These routes usually are on the wooded sides of the slopes. Wallows are another point of interest watched by hunters since mature rutting bulls primarily use them.

Mule deer rut from mid-November through early December. Their rut, though more subtle than the raucous activities of elk, is nonetheless fascinating. The bucks are constantly on the move, checking all the does in their territory daily to see when they are ready to mate. For this reason the sometimes-elusive deer are quite visible. Bucks mark their territory, by raking trees and leaving their scent from glands near their eyes. Rivals that invade the dominant buck's territory are challenged. By snorting, hissing, thrashing the brush, and raising the hair on their back, they try to make themselves appear as large and formidable as they can, but if possible they avoid actual combat in the confrontation.

Approaching a deer the savvy hunter keeps his eyes on the ground, neither looking nor moving directly towards the animal. Zigzagging back and forth the hunter is less threatening, and the deer lets him approach closer. One who hunts the same territory may learn a great deal of information that is good from one year to the next. Animals learn from their parents where to spend the summer, the winter, and other seasons. They pass the information through generations, and once they have settled on a feeding area, they are more likely to starve to death than switch.

The towering wilderness that has long resisted man's efforts to tame it, now offers him refuge from too much civilization. The Rockies, one of the last islands of American isolated wilderness, has become important for that reason. When

Trinity Lakes—Rio Grande Wilderness.

folks began to have leisure, they promptly began to misuse it and corrupt the garden we were meant to conserve as good stewards. We must recognize that what seems to be cruel and indifference to animals may be projections of the cruelty and indifference in ourselves. We must come to terms with our basic needs and preserve the means to satisfy our longing for a meaningful connection to our place on earth. So much of life takes place outdoors. Learn to enjoy it.

Always keep in mind when challenging nature on her terms that tough guys die; smart guys survive and enjoy it. One bit of survival advice for the outdoor advocate: take your spouse and family with you if they like it. Otherwise, when you return, keep your mouth shut about how much fun you had and take them out on a date they enjoy

Mental Toughness vs. Physical Toughness

Among most outdoor sporting circles the great debate between the proponents of mental toughness and those of physical toughness is sure to arise. Although neither quality is the answer in all situations, as no one person has all the answers for every situation, let me share some views on the subject. Mental discipline and toughness can accomplish many physical goals; but physical toughness by itself cannot accomplish many mental goals.

I was teaching an advanced class in Physical Education at Constantine High School in 1967. Our goal was to develop a training method that would produce a stronger, quicker, faster athlete in the shortest possible time. Most young athletes wanted to know what they could do to improve their skills for the next season. They did not have years to improve seasonal skills.

The most desired traits were strength, speed, and endurance. With this in mind we set up three methods of training: *Gymnastic Training*—the idea being that your body will gain strength faster working with its own weight rather than external weights. *Isometric Training*—exercises which tense muscles briefly in opposition to other muscles or an immovable object (the old Charles Atlas theory), or *Free Weights*—where balance and strength would be increased as opposed to strength alone with fixed weights. All the procedures followed the University of Illinois research protocol (number of repetitions, rate of progression for maximum results, etc). All participants were given a strength test assessing agility, speed, and endurance prior to starting the tests.

Keep in mind that it is a widely held belief that it takes three months to increase the size of muscle tissue, though conditioning of existing muscle can be accomplished at a rapid rate. Each group was divided into body types by height and weight. The *Free Weights* group started with seventy percent of maximum expected lift per unit, working toward ten repetitions before adding weight. At the end of three months, with weights added only at required increments, the group showed remarkable improvement using the "clean and jerk"—lifting the weight from the floor and then raising it overhead. This one lift was used for measurement because it required total body strength to accomplish the task. The one hundred forty-five pound group went from lifting 135 lbs. to 195 lbs. The one hundred fifty-four pound group improved from 135 lbs. to 205 lbs. The one hundred sixty-four pound group went from 135 lbs. to 195 lbs. The one hundred seventy-four pound group improved from 135 lbs. to 185 lbs.

All three methods of training showed similar marked improvements! Then at the end of three months all three groups took the strength test again. To me the results were impossible to believe. There was *no marked improvement* on the strength test. They couldn't jump any higher, do any more pull-

.

ups, improve their agility score, nor improve to any significant degree any strength test result!

As we evaluated the results our group came to the conclusion that we were using motivation and concentration of desire to accomplish a particular task that had very little carry-over to other tasks. We felt we were working on mental discipline and accomplishing remarkable physical tasks. The young athletes decided that to improve their football skills, or track skills, or whatever skills they desired, the *fastest* way was to mentally concentrate on that skill, mentally focus on the physical aspects of the skill. All the physical conditioning that comes with practice helps, if you have time for physical conditioning.

What does all of this have to do with enjoying the outdoors? Well, most things in life are interrelated. When I refer to the effects of altitude on a person, since people often want to know how to get in shape for the altitude in Colorado, I tell them the condition of your lungs or the iron in your muscles has little to do with your reaction to altitude. You must attack the problem mentally. The effect of hypothermia is another problem that must be attacked mentally rather than physically; learn about it before taking on the high country out West. It is as much a problem of attitude as altitude.

By "attitude" I am referring to mental focus. Regardless of your physical condition, whether you jog or smoke a pack a day, many great physical feats can be accomplished through carefully used mental powers. You may surprise yourself, but you can't fool yourself. Tough guys die, smart guys get a hold of their minds, sometimes with the help and experience of others, and enjoy many wonderful outdoor experiences, be they ordinary, or even life threatening. One cannot take on Mother Nature physically in many of the situations encountered in the wild and have pleasurable outcomes, but you can take her on using your mental as well as your physical resources and survive most situations, even learning from the encounter.

One person's hell is another person's agreeable adventure. I would rather be mentally tough than physically tough, although the first usually leads to the second. I have never been able to look at a person and decide the degree of their mental toughness. Spend a little time with them outdoors, pick their brain, and it becomes evident soon enough.

There are people who carry any pursuit to extremes, so let me include this warning about using psychological, mental toughness to prepare you for the challenges of the great outdoors. An example of mental toughness taken to the extreme led me to the brink of physical disaster, and I was not even outdoors.

During my high school teaching days I would occasionally play the role of "The Fonz" for the homecoming football assembly. Dressed like the TV character, I would ride a motorcycle into the gymnasium and give a rousing pep talk to the student body, culminating in standing backward flip dismount

"The Fonz"

from the bike. This tradition went on a few years and then was forgotten for a period of time. Years later an activity director decided the student body was ready for a return of "The Fonz." This happened shortly after my fifty-second birthday, and my wife warned me of impending doom due to my age and the degree of physical agility required for the stunt.

"Mental focus, concentration, was all I needed," I assured her. Ego might have had something to do with it, but I doubt it. It was Friday afternoon, and the show must go on. It went well enough until I attempted the back flip but didn't tuck tight enough. Coming down I hit my knee on the gym floor and knew I was in trouble. Image being everything, the act went on. Realizing I couldn't walk, a little side shuffle got me to the bike and unable to throw my leg over, in a sidesaddle mount with one leg pushing I scooted off the floor on the bike.

Knowing how upset my wife would be, and hearing her words in my head, I hobbled on one leg to a local health clinic. We had a no nonsense doctor (we called him the Vet) who would patch us up and send us on our way. I explained what had happened and told him I was going to the game that night; patch me up. The knee had water on it with major swelling, but with my apparent lack of concern (yes, I was in pain, my wife calls masculine denial) he put me on crutches. "No use in draining it now," he said, "the fluid would just come back immediately; see you Monday."

During the game I almost blacked out, and I went home early, knowing something was badly wrong. Monday the clinic doctor sent me to a specialist who had an opening on Wednesday. He took X-rays and found a broken femur, not a crack, but a break you could put a finger between.

The specialist explained to me *why* I should have been at the emergency room on Friday, *why* extremes in mental pain control are not desirable, *why* adrenalin addicts are self-destructive, and *why* the Lord gave me a brain. He operated on

Saturday, eight days after the accident. I, who had never been in the hospital in fifty-two years, had a major procedure which involved fitting the femur together with screws, was on crutches for six months, and underwent an operation a year later to remove the hardware.

It was bad, missing the fall hunting season, but rehabilitation got the leg back to where I now hike and climb in the mountains with no apparent ill effects. Yes, I believe mental focus and discipline can promote successful outcomes to many situations, but be careful in developing any technique to the extreme. Use balance and common sense. There is a fine line between being tough and being stupid. Folks build an awareness and attitude through experiences and think they have an answer for all situations. Change is a constant. Every situation varies from every other, and we must adjust to each change individually.

Our Dream Cabin

Creating something from nothing is not easy but let me assure you, most dreams can come true with a little intestinal fortitude and innovation.

Our dream: land and a cabin in the mountains.

Our problem: no money. Land in Colorado in 1994 was being gobbled up by big money from the outside. Small income people had no chance of buying mountain property with the price of land going up and up each year. In the winter of 1993 my son-in-law, Todd Richardson, and I sat around talking about this situation. A cabin in the mountains was like a cottage at the lake in other geographic areas. The scenario starts with trying to buy acreage, then an acre, then it's reduced to a lot. Buying by the square foot is coming soon.

Our solution: We found eighty acres within a reasonable distance of our homes in Montrose and placed a $500 down payment on the property with an option to buy upon visual inspection. Since it was winter we had six months before an inspection would be feasible, as the land was at 10,400-foot elevation. This parcel of mountain property was high in the mountains, surrounded by government land. No one else could build within miles of the site. It had a creek running through the middle of it, plenty of water, and a good dead-end road nearby. We could get an easement into the property and nobody would be driving by the cabin. The land backed up to the Big Blue Wilderness (over a million acres) with which we were very familiar, having ridden the area many times on horseback, enjoying the beauty and wild splendor of these mountains.

Still a problem: We needed to raise $112,000 before spring. Todd and I found six others who might be willing to form a co-op corporation and for $14,000 would own a one-eighth share of the eighty acres. Each of the members was carefully selected as to compatibility and mutual goals. That spring we all went up for a look at the property and decided a share of something now was better than little chance of ever having a place in the vanishing privately-owned wilderness.

We kept the land a year before we began to build the large cabin for all of us to use. Each share member was to put in $1,500, and we would try to build a cabin for $12,000 including materials and labor. Each member could work off part of the $1,500 by putting in labor at the rate of $5.00 an hour. Needless to say, it is hard for people, even those with good intentions, to find time to build a cabin. Since Todd and I were schoolteachers we had a greater opportunity to work during the summer. The work began that summer of 1995 and took three months of backbreaking labor, seven days a week, twelve-hour-long days, plus three hours drive time.

Todd and I worked off our shares ($1500 each) with our labor and the co-op graciously allowed us to use the cabin for outfitting during the rifle season, because we had done most of the building. The main structure was finished for a little over $8000 in materials; the rest was in labor, but still under our $12,000 goal.

Building the Cabin: When your life is the outdoors, and you plan your existence around it, you take what nature offers and make the best of it. To keep the building of an 1,800 square foot structure (counting the loft) as reasonable and economical as possible, we used standing dead Engleman Spruce cut from the property. But first we hauled an 8N Ford tractor up the mountain to snake the logs to the building site. We chained the trees to the tractor and drove as fast as we could along an old logging road, letting them spin, which de-limbed and de-barked them for the most part. We decided to use full round logs to avoid the expense of hauling them out of the mountains to be milled and then hauling them back up.

The foundation and roof were engineered for stability and snow load. A stem wall was set in place at the back and concrete pillars elevated the front. A cabin which has wind moving under it will not be troubled with snow piling up next to walls and over doors.

The logs for the walls (some logs being 34 feet long in the 28 by 34 foot structure) were lifted into place by muscle power. No crane or even block and tackle was used. For stabili-

The cabin's foundation.

ty during construction, a full log was continued through what would be window and door openings and cut in later. Each log was drilled and pinned every two feet with rebar, and butts coming together were drilled, glued and doweled to stop any air leaks. The corners were individually notched out and butted into each other for an airtight fit.

Folks we knew who were upgrading their own home's openings gave us the windows, doors, and frames. The roof was of steeply sloped metal, engineered for snow load, and provided a unique bonding experience as my son-in-law accidentally slid down one side during construction and landed on me to

The walls going up.

Kitchen duty at the cabin.

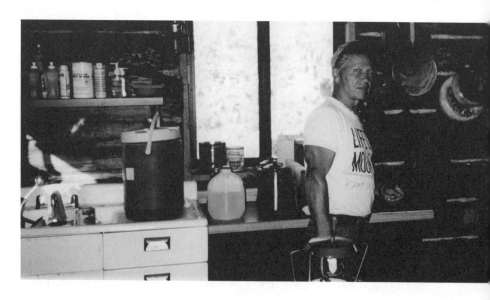

The interior.

break his twenty-foot slide and twelve foot free fall. There were also many expected and surprise episodes of rain, sleet and snow that hampered our progress.

When the main structure was complete, we added a deck and began chinking. Our formula for plastering between the logs included stapling barbed wire along the crack to which the plaster adhered and was prevented from popping

Our view.

out. Then we fashioned stairways from split logs and divided the interior space into rooms. Last we installed a wood cook stove and a Franklin stove for a fireplace.

From the completed cabin on the ridge, we appear to be alone on the vast timbered mountainside. The view in three directions is spectacular. To the north is the West Elk Wilderness (over 2 million acres); south and east is the Big Blue Wilderness (1 million acres); beyond the ridge at our back is the Uncompahgre Plateau (over 2 million acres). We did it!

The cabin is used for co-op get-togethers, and each member can use it as they will with friends. Members schedule times, but conflicting needs have not made reservations a problem over the years. We all use it for bow hunting, black powder season and summer outings at will. We all have a piece of Utopia at a small cost, and the potential of selling half a share to get our land cost back and still keeping half for the grandchildren.

At present about the only way one can purchase land inside a National Forest or Bureau of Land Management tract is to find an old logging permit or mining claim that has been handed down and is now for sale. Some are still available, and you don't need a large tract of land to build on and yet have a million-acre playground in front of you. But you need to be cautious; see "You Don't Win Them All," earlier in this book. Happy hunting.

While on the subject of building your dreams, consider the construction of the bed and breakfast lodge that follows.

The Lodge

When people like us are drawn to nature's school, her lessons influence all parts of our lives, hence when planning a lodge, we looked for the most pure and natural way to construct it. Montrose, located in a valley of southwest Colorado, is blessed with a moderately dry climate and several native building materials. With this in mind we considered log construction, stone, log and frame construction, or adobe.

Our foundation.

The walls go up.
The roof trusses go on.

Interior beams.

Our inclination was to build an adobe lodge. In talking with friends about the idea we discovered a former student who had developed an adobe brick-making machine that turned out a perfect 4 x 10 x 14-inch brick. These bricks, when compacted under hydraulic pressure, proved in rupture tests to be two and a half times stronger than regular sun-dried bricks. Another plus—we could produce them on location.

We found a local source of adobe clay and sand, which were carefully mixed to insure a body of thirty-seven percent

The finished shell.

clay. The bricks were pressed and laid in the walls while still wet. This meant they could be cut easily with no breakage. They dried while in the walls.

The foundation was poured as a monolithic slab tapered into an obelisk. A local logger cut the timbers for the lodge to special order. The headers were formed of sandwiched 2 X 10's filled with rebar and concrete held together by all-thread bars. Within nine days we put into place 7,314 bricks, each weighing fifty-four pounds. Family and friends handled all the work except the electrical installation and kitchen cabinetry. A later step was to foam the outside of the building with a polymer, which waterproofed our warm in winter, cool in summer adobe walls.

Our end result was a sound, ecological, and economically pleasing home and lodge. It encloses 3,200 square feet and

Totally finished.

has seven bedrooms with six baths. It was built for approximately one-third the cost of most custom-built residences. We still look to nature and our natural surroundings to fulfill our needs, and she has provided for us well.

The Reality Check

If you are going to spend a good deal of time in outdoor adventure, realize that nature will pull you in and challenge you to make adjustments to the basics of life, even cause you to face your own mortality sooner or later—usually when you least expect it. Know that whether you enjoy reading about outdoor adventure, watching it on television or the movies, or are capable of the adjustments of attitude to actually cope with her confrontational situations, nature will grant you gratification in your ability to solve problems, survive, and realize what you have gained from the experience. Attitude is the mind's paintbrush. Attitude can color any situation into golden delight or gloomy misery.

For one particular outing my partner, Jerry, and I had packed in a hunting camp the weekend before, then worked all week at school, sending the hunting party ahead with our wrangler on Friday. We got out of work, loaded our horses, food and gear, and traveled two hours with vehicles and trailers to a trailhead. From that point we rode most of the night, until two o'clock in the morning. At camp we slept until four, got up and fixed breakfast, packed lunches, and guided all day. That evening we packed animals out of the mountains until one o'clock Sunday morning, bedded down by two, and were up again at four working all day packing camp and animals out to the vehicles. In that country, the Rio Grande Wilderness, you must get your game and get out.

The hunters were tired, and we still had two downed elk back in the wilderness. One hunter had left his elk near a known creek covered with a blue tarp. He assured us we would have no trouble finding it, though we had not been there when he shot it. About midmorning it started to snow seriously. The wind would rob our bodies of precious heat. We told the hunters and hostler to get out of the mountains with the vehicles while they could. Jerry and I would go back for the elk.

We spent three hours walking up and down the brush-choked creek looking for an elk, not under a blue tarp, but under two feet of snow. It finally turned up, and we quartered it, dragged it back to camp where we boned the other, and began the ride over the divide. We took the direct route rather than the back way around and over as the vehicles had gone.

Riding out over the Continental Divide we witnessed one of the most beautiful views one could ever hope to see. The nearly full moon just above the horizon had turned the valleys and forests into a patchwork of midnight blue and unpolished silver. As broken clouds whisked across her face, the moon cast a lavender haze over the landscape before us. The colors of snow on the mountains shifted to shades of light blue while the spruce on the hillsides turned purple, and their shadows on the valley floor were the profoundest black. Shifting lights and prismatic colors beaming through openings in the clouds bombarded our senses. We were overwhelmed by the splendor and felt our souls stirred, as only they can be when the body is pushed to its vulnerable limits. We stopped and marveled, surrounded by the Aurora Borealis.

We arrived home at six o'clock Monday morning and went to work at seven, realizing we had slept only four hours since Friday morning.

On other occasions we have gone days with only pocket food and hot coffee, since we always stop to build a fire. Maybe you think this guide should wear a sign "WARNING: hunting with this man can be hazardous to your health!" Believe me, you will have experiences like these if spend enough time in the outdoors. When I turned sixty my wife asked me to promise I would scale back to simple summer outings, just happy family trips to the mountains.

A friend wanted to take young relatives for an elk-viewing excursion into the wilderness. The plan was for me to ride over the divide to an old hunting camp, where I'd spend a couple days scouting elk. The group was to drive 4x4s as close as possible, hike in and see elk, then hike to the lower camp. This was in August when the wilderness lies warm and alive, at least in the mind, where one imagines hidden corners for escape, thoughts of tranquil ponds among willow groves, open valleys surrounded by towering mountains undisturbed by the stress of modern society. "I'm ready!"

Off I went on my favorite horse, riding into the mountains. We had made our usual departure from Maggie Gulch north of Silverton, fifty miles from home. At the trailhead I packed a tarp, some food and light gear on the horse, and we headed out under clear sky on a beautiful day for a ride.

Within the hour, before reaching the Continental Divide, thunderclouds began forming and rolling over the peaks and into the valley. I looked back down the trail. It was an hour's ride down to timberline. Up the trail, it was ten minutes to the pass, twenty minutes crossing the crest of the divide and an hour down to the timberline on the east side of the range. My usual mindset prevailed; why turn back when you want to go forward.

Rolling over the top I faced a sheet of rain with lightning popping like firecrackers all around. I felt like *Gus* in "Lonesome Dove," dodging arrows from the Indians, only these were arrows of high voltage death. Lightning is something very much to be feared in high open country, as I knew from past experience. Lightening kills more people in Colorado than any other weather related phenomena. Dodging from ravine to rock outcropping I desperately maneuvered along the top of the divide with lightening striking all around.

My horse laid his ears back and looked at me with bulging eyes. He knew as I did, it was time to get off the mountain and out of the storm. I rode him off the trail into the cuts, and we worked our way to the bottom of the draw paralleling a rocky uplift. The ground, the horse, and I were all shuddering from earth shattering lightning strikes. I looked east and the storm continued rolling in from as far as I could see. The horse would not stand for holding over in the place I picked to wait it out. Down the mountain he scraped and skidded, dodging from one zone of limited safety to the next. After an hour of total fear and ringing eardrums, almost jumping out of the saddle with each close jolt, we entered timber.

Rigging the tarp from a deadfall at the edge of a meadow, I settled in for what would become a long two days and nights of almost continuous rain. The third night I was awakened about midnight by elk cows chirping and bulls whistling out in front of my shelter. For three hours I could hear the sounds elk make grazing and playing in the meadow before me. I couldn't see them in the dark, and a light would have started a stampede, but for three hours there was entertainment all around.

That morning three hikers made it to the upper camp and we followed tracks around the timber and up above the tree line. We counted 136 elk with more drifting in and out of timber. What a wonderful observation of nature.

The guests stayed two hours and went back to the lower camp to be with the others. It rained again that night and all the next day. So, after four days and nights spent mostly huddling under a tarp in the rain, I pulled out for home. If a person does not come home from a trip to the high country a better person, he is doing something wrong. Dedication, grit, heart, whatever you call what's inside a person, can only be measured by trials. Nature provides those tests and helps you know that no one can label you a looser if you are able to grow from your experiences. You can't learn without some failures. Being able to accept this and view them as temporary setbacks helps you become a winner when it counts. All of us, especially young people, need to know that there is sufficient reward in life for succeeding simply at the level of doing one's best.

Perhaps my wife won't read this book; she has spent enough sleepless nights. I'll probably continue to enjoy outdoor adventure as I hope others will, realizing that we deal with nature on her terms. Set your course and go for it, seizing every minute of life as if it might be your last.

The Ultimate Hunt

It was September 8, 2001 and I had finally won the draw. I had applied each year for ten years for a muzzle loading permit for bull elk in Area 61 before receiving the much sought after hunting permit. After outfitting for almost thirty years, this would be my chance, at sixty-one years young to have a quality hunt for myself.

In Colorado you can apply for preference points for special hunting areas and wait for a draw. The more points, the better your chance for success in the draw. This was a long awaited permit to hunt bull elk with a muzzleloader in a trophy area. With knowledge of the area spanning thirty years I felt sure of collecting a fine trophy bull.

My cousin, John Chappell, was coming from Michigan to enjoy the hunt with me in the Uncompahgre Plateau in southwest Colorado. He decided to come out by bus, so he would have time to enjoy the ride and anticipate the adventure ahead of him. We are alike in that we look less to creature comforts than to adventure. He could well afford a plane ticket, but he figured the ride cross-country would be part of the great experience. He arrived in Montrose with all of his gear strapped to a plastic sled, which had started many conversations along the way with folks who wondered why he was going to Colorado in September with a sled. He would explain that it was to drag the elk out of the mountains. Well, we all have our peculiar ideas of how to make a hunt more pleasurable.

Was it too late for a couple of men in their sixties, with different backgrounds and experiences to share an enjoyable, quality hunt? It's never too late! Nothing happens too late in life, if one is not too old to love it.

Our lodging would be a cabin on a knoll looking across four miles to the mountain. We could have driven around and up the hill arriving at the high plateau on the other side in about fifteen minutes, but we chose to walk uphill for two hours each morning, carrying thirty-five pounds of equipment. Mother Nature might sprinkle us with adversity, so we had to be ready with every needed article in our packs. Why climb the mountain each day? Only a dead fish goes downstream all the time. To enjoy and learn from an experience sometimes one has to swim upstream. Don't take the easiest route all the time; climb that mountain!

Our plan for hunting each day was derived from the experiences we had while walking. In mid-September we knew the rut would be getting into high gear, and the bugle call of a bull elk is the wildest sound of the outdoors. I've heard wolves and mountain lions, almost all the calls of predators, and testosterone-charged animals, but a bull elk bugling is the wildest of all, and best heard from outside of house or truck. The gift of wildlife is best accepted out there among them. As we walk we feel the chill of coming winter and know it is the greatest killer of all—not hunting. Hunters conserve and manage, and by supporting game wardens and wildlife biologists, control populations of animals. This has been proven by the comeback of the once endangered elk and other threatened species.

"*Be Prepared*" is not only the Boy Scout's motto, it should be that of the modern hunter who wants to use the "smoke pole" (muzzle loading rifle). Not only does the hunter need some new approaches found by scouting the area, he needs to prepare his weapon and keep it ready. Here are some tips I have learned along the way.

Carry and use solvent to dissolve and remove powder fouling. You can use vegetable shortening for a lubricant. Loading the black powder rifle with a greasy lubricant and firing it "cures" the bore, and hot water will re-cure the barrel after later firings. Today's black powder produces less residue or fouling, but never use anything but 100% cotton patches as synthetic fibers can melt and fuse to the barrel. Don't ask why, but I prefer a conical bullet.

A ball discharger is a handy piece of equipment allowing you to unload your rifle at the end of each day's hunt, and pipe cleaners are extremely useful for cleaning a muzzleloader's flash channel. Every day, clean the channel and bore with *hot water,* which facilitates drying. Reload fresh powder every morning. In wet weather I put a balloon over the muzzle; the balloon presents no problem when the gun is fired, and prevents condensation or precipitation from getting into the piece. Refuel the flash channel now and then, since powder settles as you trek along.

You have prepared your firearm, so now prepare your mind. Having a plan when you hunt eases the mind. Work on your patience and enjoy working the plan, rather than just walkin' around huntin'. What for hunters is just an interesting charade is for the hunted a matter of life and death. Game animals are constantly aware of their surroundings. Wonder why they are so skittish? We're trying to shoot them! Maneuvering through an area, hunters will alert any critter within a quarter of a mile, but with favorable wind, and early morning or darkness you can proceed unnoticed. Get there early; have a plan!

A bull elk will spend the night nosing around places where cows feed. Shortly after daybreak he will follow a group of cows out of their grazing area into the cover where the cows will bed. If none are close to their estrus peak, the bull will quickly loose interest and be on the move again. His course may take him to another bedding area. Mid-day is usually the shifting time for the bulls. Hunters can take a short nap mid-morning and mid-afternoon, but stay awake during mid-day. Don't gather with your buddies to discuss what you saw that morning; get out and hunt! Spend the time on the ridges in oak brush where bedding takes place—not in open woodlots. Stay until dark. Most elk activity is during the night, but mid-day is a time for bulls moving. A bull in rut doesn't sleep much, just a rest in mid-morning and mid-afternoon and then they run all night. Get to your hunt area early before other hunters and leave after they depart. Hunt and rest all through the day, like your prey.

Our hunt would start each morning at 3:30 without the use of an alarm clock. Most anyone can train himself or herself to wake up whenever they want. The brain is always working and aware of time, so we woke ourselves at that hour. When I was in education and teaching psychology we conditioned rats to run mazes and even mealworms to run through a maze. I figure our brain is as trainable as a mealworm's.

We never talked about enjoying the experience, but I think John and I knew we would be about as happy as we made up our minds to be in whatever we do. We tend not to get bogged down in other people's problems. We control only one life, and if we do it well, it rubs off and enriches other folks' lives. One of my mottos is "Don't pole-vault over peas," meaning you save your big guns for your big wars. Stress is caused by the accumulation of little things in life not the major big ones. Nobody controls our happiness but us. Constantly clear, focus, and train the mind; and then communicate good things to others. The uncluttered mind is what you need to enjoy life and the outdoors.

Opening day we spent listening and sensing the pattern for the hunt. We spotted three bulls, heard others whistling and bugling, and concentrated on understanding their movements. I took no shots though there were numerous bulls in the area. At the end of the day we compared notes and talked about the next day's hunt plan.

The second day we were sure the rut was moving into full activity for the bulls. We spotted several cows being pushed by younger bulls, but we could hear the larger bulls calling from the high points. They would come down and claim their harem at night.

The third day the air vibrated with the piercing calls of bulls screaming at the top of their lungs, but not moving. Walking down off the mountain after dark we were passed by bulls running and bugling all around us. We estimated there were eight bulls moving on our side of the mountain that night. This evening, we figured, was two days away from full rut. So, the fourth day we went home and had breakfast in civilization with my wife since we were only an hour and a half from the ranch.

It is good to take a break from hunting. Sharing the experience with friends and family makes it all the more satisfying. Get your family involved; though the hunt may take you away from them for a time, it is important to share what you are getting out of it. Even if it is only with stories and mental images, it is good to bring them along. We spent breakfast talking and sharing the wonders of the wilderness. Then we turned on the news that September 11th morning. The attacks and disaster in the East brought home the transience and fragility of our lives, but made it all the more important to enjoy each day we are given. Not to minimize the horror of the event, but life must go forward; so we spent the night with family and went back up to camp with a greater appreciation of why we live each day with reverence. Life is an adventure, a trip into the uncertain freedom of our world.

Thursday the rut, that primal surge of nature, opened full bore. Bulls screamed all around us. This was one of the most indescribable experiences of my life. No shots were fired, and I waited one more day for the ultimate hunt.

Friday I was to go after the biggest bull. We knew where he was early in the morning with his eleven cows high on a ridge of scrub oak brush. Long before daylight I was a hundred yards below him, listening to him run back and forth along a trail through the brush around his harem. Since he was vigilantly guarding the herd, it would be hard to get much closer without being noticed. In the first light of predawn I could see him trotting from one side of the knoll to the other, warning other bulls to stay away. The oak brush was thick, and he was moving constantly; I could not get a clear shot.

Reviewing my own considerations for a successful hunt, I knew mistakes, as in all sports, tend to lose games. I thought to myself:
Use passive calling, chirping, but don't call loudly or too often.
Scout the area.
Don't do what (or go where) everyone else does.
Don't take the easy way.
Don't chase a bugling elk, intercept it.
Know the area. It takes planning to be in the right place at the right time.

Weather should not stop the hunter.

Travel as far as your legs can take you; practice walking to get in shape.

Mistakes include shooting at game out of range, not camouflaging face and hands, moving too often, or taking a buddy along—hunt alone.

Below me another bull was moving toward the knoll with his harem. I dropped down and waited for him to cross below me, knowing he would not come too close to the other bull. He brought his eight cows fifty yards below, screaming at the other bull constantly. Evidently he was taking the cows from a bedding area in the lower ground to a higher vantage point. He was a nice five point with symmetrical tines on each side, but I judged him to be smaller than the bull above me, so I let him go.

Now concentrating on the bull above, I chirped quietly and tried to sound like a horny straggler from the passing group. The bull ran back and forth watching and snuffing but would not come down. I could see his body occasionally but the oak brush would not afford an open shot. Next I rubbed a limb against a tree, pretending to be a bull thrashing the brush, but he refused to investigate.

The next plan was to move uphill and get closer, since noise did not seem to bother him in his frenzy. Moving slowly up the hill, I noted a slight breeze, but it was moving across my intended course, not up the hill—perfect. I could now see the path he had been running on, but no elk. Then a doe appeared on the path with her yearling. Crouching down, I let them pass, knowing I would have to wait five minutes to let her move well away. Waiting, listening to the bull crash the brush, I felt he would surely be back along the trail any minute. Slowly I moved one step closer to the trail for that perfect shot.

To my right there was a loud whistle from the doe that had come back up the trail to watch me. The whole area exploded with elk charging every which way, and in a few minutes they were gone, leaving only the silence ringing in my ears.

Going back down the mountain I met with John, shared the experience, and told him we were leaving as I had promised four other buddies I would take them on a bow hunt the next morning. Was I disappointed that I waited ten years and ten minutes to have the ultimate trophy hunt, worked seven days to reach the time of full rut, and was now walking away? No, this was one of the most enjoyable hunts I had ever been on. We had seen elk, turkey, even a bear, and would have great memories. The goal is to enjoy the outdoors not the kill. On to the bow hunt, which would be another adventure with four good people. Was it a successful hunt? Yes, and that one and other hunts may be in another book.

I have taken many hunters into remote wilderness areas, and to faraway cabins with creature comforts. They often come expecting the vicarious experiences they read about in outdoor magazines—hunts that don't normally happen. Sometimes it

Cousin, John Chappell, helping to break a young horse.

turns out just as they expected, though fifty percent of the time they are ready to come out after three days, tired and dejected, ready to pay the full price, but also ready to say they went on a great hunt and go home. Most of these hunters have not developed the mental attitude prior to the hunt necessary to fully enjoy the experience. Over the winter they dream about the next great hunt, but in the fall they repeat the same scenario. I hope that this little book helps the reader prepare for a truly successful hunt. Pay your dues, be a part of the game, enjoy each day and the memories they build. You don't win them all, but you can take pleasure in every adventure you survive in this life. This is a lesson we must teach the next generation who are too often charmed by virtual realities.

Son's first fish.

Son and daughter (Sherri) backpacking the San Juans.

Summation

I mentioned at the beginning of this book that life's lessons are learned from experiences in the outdoors; here are some thoughts and conclusions, some derived from experience and some from listening to others.

Nature is a powerful force, and life's demands on a human are also powerful. Both can be relentless, and unyielding in their insistence. Life's needs change from hour to hour like the weather; there are no guarantees. One does not go through life without storms; at least on the horizon there is grief or even tragedy. If there is any such thing as "freedom" or "choice" there is also chance.

Don't look for easy answers or simple formulas, but if you learn from mistakes you gain a priceless education.

There is a big difference between "making a living" and "making a life." The material things you want don't amount to anything; more money will build nothing in your character of value. With each toy you buy there is one more link in the chain around your neck. The pursuit of happiness is not a chase after wealth.

Much of the meaning and importance of life addresses our need to value ourselves and be honored by others. When life's temptations lure you from the path of honor, you must be sure of your coordinates. Your compass should point you toward respect and a high regard for the dignity of others. Duty

Alaskan Sockeye fishing out of Saldotna.

Halibut fishing out of Homer Alaska.

Top of Mt. Sneffles, highest mountain in the Sneffles Range (14,250 ft.) I climbed it because it was there!

demands that you sacrifice for what is right against whatever odds.

This discussion brings me to the subject of marriage. Men must look at our primal instincts, our striving for success at

Going south for the winter.

work. Centering on work is okay, but not at the price of failure at home. The best gift a father can give his children is the example of love, honor and respect for his wife, their mother. There may be little of the feminine emotion in a man, nor nothing of the masculine drives in most women; but one can appreciate the differences in each. And what fun it is to try and understand these differences. My wife and I often talk of killing each other but never about divorce. I give thanks and credit to the one who has put up with me for the last forty years. She entered my world, and I wish I could as easily enter hers.

Rafting the Colorado River with my wife.

Time is worth much more than money; so don't waste yours or anybody else's. Happiness is being too busy to have time to make other people miserable.

The enjoyment of the outdoors seems to replace the need for medicines. It appears the more medical attention people can afford the more they need it, and the amount of medicine it takes for people to survive is directly related to the amount of affluence they have. Outdoor oriented people are comfortable with the bare necessities; they seem to develop a less demanding life and a lower comfort range.

In order to enjoy the outdoors you set out on a trail to proficiency, developing the skills that lead you to a destination, but not always in a straight line. Also you learn not to resurrect the boogieman; he is with you all the time anyway, in the dark caves of your mind.

Just a summer outing.

I do not seem to be a fortunate man when it comes to obtaining the riches of the world, but I consider myself wealthy. At this time I am retired, and though I look busy, I am probably just confused. I spend time in the mountains inspired by the pure air, rarified by trees of the forest, and I think about this time in my life. I notice the birds moving south to escape the ravages of winter. I think they know something that I am slowly coming to believe. So, I live in Colorado in the summer and fall and follow the birds south to Texas in the winter, where my wife and I can fish and enjoy the outdoors. We have explored the Baja of California to the south and Alaska in the north, completing our visit to all the states of the union.

Our winter home in the Hill Country of Texas.

Playing tennis wish my daughter, Lori, in Houston, Texas.

Sheephead fishing off the jetty at Padre Island, South Texas.

I still participate in specialty hunts and cook at the outfitting camps. I enjoy giving the guests two choices for supper: take it or leave it. I spend as much time as I can in the mountains and outdoors, and I watch the folks coming to nature to fill the voids in their lives. They come carrying the stuff of their other world, and destroy the peace and simplicity they came for. The quest for utopia, the perfect life, will destroy you unless you are willing to choose the basics. Creature comforts are enjoyable, but they lead you to believe you need more and more, speed and power, ease and luxury.

There is a reason that folks always look back in time, realizing that the happiest times of their lives were when they had little but were working to get ahead. When people have too much money, power, or things, they become decadent; they regress and lose vigor. Empires have decayed, and great civiliza-

Family fishing in Colorado.

tions have collapsed, when they became too comfortable. The end of total comfort and relaxation is death. When one chooses a luxury cruise and shopping in duty-free ports over a hunt and a sleeping bag under the stars, an attitude is created about oneself and the world around you. I can afford a motorhome as big as a Greyhound bus, but I prefer a more modest way to enjoy traveling. I can afford bill fishing in the Bahamas, but I know a hike in the mountains and trout caught from the nearby stream will do me more good.

The desire for more things and comforts is constantly sold to us Americans, And it has changed our outlook on life, it has changed our bodies when we look in the mirror, and it has

A beautiful sunset.

changed our minds about the people around us. The world is fine; the people tend to mess it up; but we need to laugh at our mistakes, learn from them, and enjoy the differences in people rather than fight over them.

My father always said, "What you *are* is more important than what you *do*." Character counts more than occupation. Though he was always a hard worker, skilled and respected for his good work as carpenter and machinist, he chose to characterize himself as a neighbor and family man who could be counted on. His life must have given him peace of mind; he

Raising Norwegian Fjord horses, Montrose, Colorado.

slept good, had a good appetite, and loved the outdoors. At this writing he is ninety-six and still putting along.

I believe the Lord doesn't take days away from you that are spent enjoying the outdoors. In return He gives you the blessings of a contented mind, one of the greatest gifts any person can have.

Live your dream!